THOUGHTS ENCOURAGING **YOU** TO THINK

STUDY TO SHOW YOURSELF APPROVED

NEIL FICHTHORN

WestBow
PRESS®
A DIVISION OF THOMAS NELSON
& ZONDERVAN

WestBow Press books may be ordered through booksellers or by contacting:

WestBow Press
A Division of Thomas Nelson & Zondervan
1663 Liberty Drive
Bloomington, IN 47403
www.westbowpress.com
844-714-3454

ISBN: 979-8-3850-4542-6 (sc)
ISBN: 979-8-3850-4543-3 (e)

Library of Congress Control Number: 2025904464

Print information available on the last page.

WestBow Press rev. date: 03/21/2025

ACKNOWLEDGEMENTS

Just after I retired, my good friend Dr. Bill Welte, retired CEO of America's Keswick, asked me to write three devotionals for a book he planned to publish. The thought was very discomforting because I hated writing throughout college and had no idea what to write. But I sent three, and that started it all. Since then, I have written over 400 devotionals and have a mailing list of over 250 that receive them weekly.

Initially, I would ask various people to proofread one for me, but that got laborious. My daughter, Pam, trained as an Executive Secretary, did them for a short time but had to stop because of her busy work schedule and home responsibilities with two girls and a husband.

Then a God-thing happened: my wife's cousin in Oregon said she would proofread each one and did so for several years. Thank you, Esther Knaupp. Your contribution to this book is significant.

During all of this time, my daughter, Pamela Keller, was experiencing two things: relief from home pressure and the beginning of her own ministry, leading women in reading through the Bible. She has studied herself to be a theologian! And she is now using not only her secretarial skills but also making valuable comments on most devotionals. Thank you so much, Pam. This would be impossible without you. And I know you are busier than ever, but you are also committed to helping me.

I also thank my wife, Mary Esther, for the times she has proofed something and said, "You can't send that!" She has more delicate, tender sensitivities than I do. And I am always thankful I listened to her because she was correct. Thanks also for her patience as I spent untold hours at the computer thinking, writing, rewriting, formatting, organizing, etc.

This book would be impossible without the help of my son-in-law, David Macbeth, a computer expert. He has helped me with hundreds of issues that I could not figure out. He is the most patient man I know. I thank you sincerely.

I offer many thanks to my dear friend Phil Burks, who has assisted me financially in making this book possible.

Thanks also to about a dozen or so of my devotional readers who respond frequently to encourage or share insights I had not considered.

ENDORSEMENTS

"Here is a unique challenge to think more deeply about an array of teachings you have probably assimilated but never truly tested. Neil Fichthorn will guide you to new convictions and a more vibrant application of God's Word in your daily experience. This is more than a mere collection of devotionals. It is a dynamic handbook for making your life in the Lord more effective."– Ron Blue, Retired Professor, Dallas Theological Seminary

"Neil Fichthorn wants you to think, to re-evaluate your beliefs and examine those you thought were wrong. His goal of getting you to think drives you to the Scriptures to find the sure foundation for your beliefs. Some of your long-held beliefs will be challenged while others will be confirmed. Get ready to think! – Dr. Woodrow Kroll, President and Senior Bible Teacher, Back to the Bible (retired).

"As I began to compose my opinion of Neil Fichthorn's excellent book entitled, "Thoughts Encouraging You to Think," it occurred to me that my thoughts had already been perfectly stated long ago by none other than the great Philosopher Socrates who said- "KNOW THYSELF...THE UNEXAMINED LIFE IS NOT WORTH LIVING". Neils' book will masterfully stimulate his readers to do just that- to carefully examine their personal beliefs in order to better understand themselves and others."–Dr. Kenneth Markley-Retired Psychologist

"It is a privilege to endorse the devotions written by Neil Fichthorn. He is a friend from the days when we served together on the Back to the Bible Board of Trustees in Lincoln, Nebraska. I benefit by reading his devotionals that are written to make you think. No matter what your religious or spiritual background, if you have been caused to think by reading his devotionals, he has achieved his goal. You will be challenged to think about your walk with Jesus as you read his writing." –Harold J. Berry, D.D, Lincoln, Nebraska

"For more than 51 years, my mentor and friend has taught me to THINK. He has stretched my heart and mind to THINK and look past legalism and beyond. I am thankful for his influence and pray you will now read his thoughts with an open heart. THINK will change your life." –Dr. Bill Welte, CEO and retired Director of America's Keswick, is presently Executive Director of Advancement.

Unless otherwise noted, all scripture is from the New International Version (NIV).

CONTENTS

INTRODUCTION

If you know some of my background, you will understand my thoughts much better if you read this introduction. I highly suspect I am a tad like you.

I am an overly educated person with average intellect. Even with a master's degree in music education, I snuck in with every shortcut possible. My only formal Bible training was several Bible courses in a Christian Liberal Arts College. I never attended Bible College or seminary.

I have been involved in Christian music for more than sixty years, but I do not have a great voice or play any instrument well. I am, however, an excellent choir director.

So, what qualifies me to write a book?

I was involved in all levels of the Bible Conference ministry for five decades. I was a conference director for fifteen years, a second man in line for ten years, and in leadership positions for summer seasons at lower-level positions for twenty-five years. I was also a church choir director for more than forty years. During those combined years, I heard some of the finest, best-known speakers of the day and took voracious notes. I can go to my note files, which are like a concordance! I ate many meals with these people and had many in my home. This gave me many opportunities to discuss the theological questions I had.

With that average background, how could I be a highly successful conference director? I was instrumental in completely turning around two conferences, one from old age, the other from financial disaster in the millions. How do I explain that apart from the Lord? Common street sense. I never did anything brilliant or revolutionary. I just put into practice common sense.

But perhaps you need to know that my involvement in colleges, churches, and conference ministries was exceptionally conservative, some to the degree of extreme legalism. No one forced me to stay, and I loved my ministry, but I always had unanswered questions about the Christian life, not theology as such. Getting answers to those questions always led to the same conclusion: I didn't wholly buy into man-made, extra-biblical answers.

When I retired as a Bible Conference director in 2000 and was no longer living in a glass house, I began to think about determining what I could ascertain from the scripture instead of what men told me or expected of me. I started to have new Christian friends (we moved several times) and acquaintances. I did conference consulting in ministries that did not follow the same conservative theological path I had trod but loved Jesus just as much.

One day, a friend asked me to compose several devotionals for his edited book. I had no idea what to write. If there was one thing in my educational career I hated, it was writing.

So, I began thinking. That changed my life. It opened the possibility of untold subjects I had questioned through the years. This book is composed of some of those devotionals.

Maybe you can relate to that in some capacity.

Now, I write for one reason: to make you think. I want to rock your boat, stir your thinking, and challenge many things my strain of conservative Christianity has unquestionably accepted over the years.

This book uses devotionals that deal with real-life, day-to-day issues where the rubber meets the road. Little of the book has deep theological subjects, for I am not a theologian. As I was in conference leadership using primarily common sense and street smarts, I approached daily Christian life issues, one issue at a time, using a verse or two instead of 10-25 verses that essentially say the same thing. I diligently try to give real-life examples from my own experiences. Be aware that I purposely do not name names of individuals or organizations when I am stating negative things. I hope you will not assume that I have conjured up the illustration; be assured that I am attempting to avoid demeaning that person or organization since they will not have the opportunity to respond. I will keep it as factual as possible, remembering that some of these matters go back to as much as 75 years.

I don't expect you to agree with everything I write. If you disagree, I encourage you to prove your position correct through research, study, and prayer. If you think for yourself and come up with a different conclusion, you will have achieved your goal and mine.

I have grown more in the past three years because of writing these thoughts than in 50 years of being force-fed from the pulpit.

Finally, if you disagree and can't find help, I always encourage your comments. I want to continue growing spiritually, especially in my daily walk with Jesus. Teach me but be nice. I pay close attention to them and use them for further information, scrutiny, and wisdom in future writing.

While this book is organized into chapters, its format easily allows for daily reading, one section of a chapter at a time. The Table of Contents will help you make sense of that.

CHAPTER

1

THE BIBLE

Any writing or study must have a firm foundation, a starting point, and a cornerstone.

This book is only about what the Bible teaches us about doctrine and holy living. It is specifically designed to challenge your thinking. My thoughts are no more inspired than those who have taught and preached for decades. But I believe that any true believer who does not study the scriptures and decides on his own what they mean is, at the least, lazy.

So, let's begin at the beginning and decide to think.

A. WHY I BELIEVE THE BIBLE IS GOD'S INSPIRED WORD AND WITHOUT ERROR.

1. Its unity. It contains 66 books written by 30 authors in three languages, in different countries, and on every social plane of its time. Yet, all are without disagreement or contradiction. Sometimes, people are called by other names, just as they are today… nicknames. Some facts are slightly different because of the author's perspective, just as today, people witnessing an auto accident from different angles give a different perspective. But the issue is true, and the reports are accurate.
2. Fulfilled prophecy. The numerous fulfilled prophecies further evidence the Bible's divine inspiration. Over 300 prophecies in the story of Jesus's birth and life have come to pass. Additionally, many prophecies about Jesus's return, which have

either been fulfilled or are currently unfolding, further validate the Bible's divine inspiration. In the Old Testament, prophets repeatedly made predictions: some were fulfilled within the prophet's lifetime, others years or centuries later, precisely as predicted. None were left unfilled. No other holy book has prophecy of this kind.

3. The Bible's enduring influence and resilience against attacks further prove its divine inspiration. Since its inception, the Bible has shaped the lives of millions every year, making it the best-selling book of all time. Despite numerous attempts to eradicate it, the Bible stands strong, facing attacks from all sides. This resilience is a testament to its divine origin. Other holy books offer truth AND error. The Bible is without error.

4. Its inexhaustible depth and, at the same time, its simplicity. Nothing has been added in 1800 years, yet it speaks accurately on every subject. Archeology proves its historical accuracy. When it speaks of things scientifically, it has not been disproven. The more you read it, the more you learn. It is superior to all human wisdom. Yet, it is simple enough for those with child-like understanding and the uneducated. Illiterate people can understand it when it is read and explained to them. Savages have been utterly transformed into their own healthy culture.

5. The character of those who believe it is compared to those who do not. This is not mass acceptance of those who believe it or condemnation of those who do not. But in unmistakable general terms, who are good, honest, morally upright, law-abiding people? Which ones cause dissension and upheaval and fill the jails? Which fills the churches?

6. It is truthful. All the Bible's heroes had faults, some grievous sins. The Bible does not cover this up; instead, it demonstrates its truthfulness and teaches us through it. It confirms that "all have sinned."

7. It's miracles. These things cannot be humanly explained: instant healing, walking on water, people raised from the dead, feeding thousands with just enough food for one person, etc. All of these have eyewitness accounts.

8. It's martyrs—people currently and hundreds of thousands through written history who have not recanted their trust in Christ when given the opportunity. Yes, some would die for a cause today, but in most cases, they have some mental maladjustment. Which of them would die burned at the stake or sawn in two?

9. The testimony of Jesus Himself. Jesus quotes dozens of Old Testament scriptures, confirming His belief in the scriptures available to Him during His lifetime.

A simple song says it in a nutshell: "God said it, I believe it, and that settles it for me."

B. OUR VIEW OF THE BIBLE

Do I believe the Bible is totally accurate and without error? When I find difficult passages, do I research for an answer that satisfies my soul? When my mind still cannot grasp God's ways, do I trust by faith or waver in my convictions?

Am I willing to accept that God's ways are not always my ways and that He knows the beginning from the end, that somehow, some way, some time, I will understand what He does and why? Do I realize that if I knew all the answers, I would be like God and not need a God?

Now the question is, am I more godly if I read straight through the Bible every year or if I regularly seek passages that relate to my needs, answer my questions, and affect my life? Is reading sufficient, or must there be accompanying thought, study, and application? Does reading daily devotionals written by those who have studied a passage and related it to a real-life situation have any compensatory value? Generally, am I more inclined to remember a passage because it is today's reading or a passage well explained by a living illustration? Is the issue reading or comprehension and application?

Does the process of Bible engagement make me more godly, or does the time spent doing it, however I do it, make me more godly? How do I rate using those criteria?

I strongly encourage you to check out this website from Back to the Bible. It offers a variety of choices for daily Bible contact. They are exceptionally well done. At least check it out!

https://mail.google.com/mail/u/0/#inbox/FMfcgzGmvTrlCHTGBnmRzfBSbNltVVbd

C. IS JESUS THE ONLY WAY TO HEAVEN?

There was a time when nearly all people in our Western culture shared the same general worldview. America had a spiritual environment in which religion flourished as it did in no other Western country. In time, the post-moderns threw out absolute truth and replaced it with "tolerance," a vague word of indeterminate meaning, which they applied selectively at the expense of the Christian worldview.

"Tolerance" used to mean "bearing or putting up with someone or something not especially liked." However, now the word has been redefined to "all values, all beliefs, all lifestyles, all truth claims are equal." Denying this makes a person "intolerant" and thus worthy of contempt. We are told that for the sake of unity, we are not to draw any definitive lines or declare any absolutes. Doctrinal issues once painted black and white are now seen as gray.

Paul forewarned us that this time would come when he wrote: "For the time will come when people will not put up with sound doctrine. Instead, to suit their own desires, they will gather around them a great number of teachers to say what their itching ears want to hear. They will turn their ears away from the truth and turn aside to myths." (II Tim. 4:3-4).

In this age of tolerance where absolutes are rejected, it is difficult for many to accept a position of finality with no escape clause. The Bible clearly teaches several things that are unacceptable to the "tolerant." Consider:

1. All have sinned. (Romans 3:23) All means all. That means you. God hates sin–all sin: little "white lies," stealing, adultery, murder, etc. No matter how good you are, you are not perfect, and God demands perfection. (Matthew 5:48) We can never gain perfection on our own, but when receiving Christ as Savior we are told that His righteousness is credited to us. (Romans 4:1-7)
2. Sin separates us from God. (Isaiah 59:2)
3. There is only one way into heaven: Jesus. (John14:6; Romans 6:23; Acts 4:12) Jesus said so himself. He cannot be passed over merely as a good man. Making a statement that He is the only way to heaven is either true, or it makes Him a liar or a lunatic, not a good man!
4. If Jesus is the only way, that eliminates other ways some people want to claim: good deeds outweighing bad deeds, buying your way in (giving time and money for "God's purposes"), or thinking that you are better than someone else (comparing your life to someone of lesser character). (Romans 11:5,6; Titus 3:5).
5. Other religions are false. Being sincere is not enough! Dr. Ravi Zacharias, a Christian apologist who lectured in academic and religious circles around the world, is an expert on other religions. He says: "Christianity is not the only religion that claims exclusivity. For instance, Muslims radically claim exclusivity–not just theologically, but also linguistically. Muslims believe that the sole, sufficient and consummate miracle of Islam is the Koran. They say, however, it's only recognizable in Arabic and that any translation desacralizes it. And it's not just a basic understanding

of Arabic that is required, but a sophisticated knowledge of the language. As for Buddhism, it was born when Gautama Buddha rejected two fundamental assertions of Hinduism-the ultimate authority of the Vedas, which are their scriptures, and the caste system. Hinduism itself is very uncompromising on two or three issues: the law of the karma, which is the law of moral cause and effect, so that every birth is a rebirth that makes recompense for the previous life; the authority of the Vedas; and reincarnation. Hinduism claims it is a very tolerant faith. What that really means is that Hinduism allows you to practice your own religion so long as it fits into their notion of truth which is syncretistic (attempts to blend different or even opposing beliefs). As for Sikhism, it came as a challenge to both Hinduism and Buddhism. Then there are the atheists-they reject the viewpoints of anyone who believes in God. And even Baha'ism, which claims to be the cosmic embrace of all religions, ends up excluding the exclusivists! Therefore, the statement that Christians are arrogant by claiming exclusivity ignores the reality that every other major religion does so as well."

The Bible is not only the *final* authority on spiritual matters; it is the only authority. Times have changed, but the Bible is not outdated. In fact, the longer it's around and archeology continues its discoveries, the more the Bible is corroborated. Where history and science are concerned, the Bible has yet to be proven incorrect; on the contrary, science changes as it discovers more; the Bible does not! History is updated, not outdated!

All of the rationalizations that man can make to avoid the simple fact that Jesus is the only way fall short of the truth. The Bible clearly teaches that Satan blinds our eyes (II Corinthians 4:4), man thinks more highly of himself than he should (Romans 12:3), and there is a way that seems right to man, but the result is spiritual death (Proverbs 14:12).

Jesus is the only way of salvation since He is the only One who can forgive our sins because of His sinlessness (Romans 6:23). No other religion teaches the depth or seriousness of sin and its consequences. No other religion offers the infinite payment of sin that only Jesus Christ could provide. No other "religious founder" was God become man (John 1:1,14). Jesus had to be God so that He could pay our sin-debt. Jesus had to be a man so He could die. Salvation is available only through faith in Jesus Christ! "Salvation is found in no one else, for there is no other name under heaven given to men by which we must be saved" (Acts 4:12).

Reject this to your own peril!

D. ARE ALLAH AND JEHOVAH THE SAME GOD?

Recently, I had a discussion with a Christian gentleman who stated that Allah and Jehovah are the same God. I was quite surprised. I know almost nothing about the Muslim religion; I have never read even a full page of the Quran. So, I decided to check it out based on what the Quran says.

First, both religions claim their scriptures are inspired. On this, there is no debate. Since they are vitally different, how can they both represent the same "god"?

Secondly, the Quran states that Allah has no son: "It is specified in the Quran that Allah has no son." The Bible says Jehovah has a Son, Jesus, our Savior. Among many other differences that I discovered, this one was enough to help me determine that they could not be the same "god."

Here are some quotes from the Quran:

"In the Muslim tradition, there are 99 names of God. Not one of these names refers to Allah as Father. In fact, the Quran teaches that Allah is the Mighty (3:6) and Most Holy (59:23; 62:1) but does not mention Allah in a familial-type relationship as in Christianity." So I typed in the question, does Allah have a son? There were numerous choices and the one I chose gave many translations (paraphrases) of the same verse. I have chosen this one: Mohsin Khan's translation of Chapter (17) sūrat l-isrā (The Night Journey): "And say: 'All the praises and thanks be to Allah, Who has not begotten a son (nor an offspring), and Who has no partner in (His) Dominion, nor He is low to have a Wali (helper, protector or supporter). And magnify Him with all the magnificence, [Allahu-Akbar (Allah is the Most Great)]." (This translation is apparently akin to our Amplified Bible.) That alone is enough to tell us that the god of Islam is not the same as the God of the Bible. How many times in the Bible is Jehovah referred to as our Father and Jesus as His Son?

That introduces us to a third issue: Is Allah a "god" of peace?

The Bible teaches again and again that Christianity is a religion of peace. Jesus said, among many other things, "Peace I leave with you; my peace I give you." (John 14:27) Is Allah a god of peace? Are we not seeing in the news virtually every day the atrocities committed by Muslims in the name of Allah? Are these all radicals? If so, what is the general Muslim population doing to contain or even condemn them? Every now and then we will see something in the news which a radical Christian perpetuated, perhaps at an abortion clinic. It is followed immediately by the denunciation from the vast majority of Christians. Not so with the Muslims.

From a website commenting on Islam, "Islam is not a religion of peace. Islam has been around long enough for tradition and family to condemn future generations to that religion, but make no mistake, Islam is still conversion by the sword. It is still a religion which kills those who reject it." Does that sound like the God of the Bible?

Dozens of websites assert that Islam considers Israel to be "The Little Satan" and the United States as "The Great Satan." Other claims include:

- "It's a religion that calls for the extermination of 'infidels' outside of their faith, specifically, Jews and Christians. It's a religion that calls on its soldiers to shout 'Allahu Akbar' ('God is Great' in Arabic) as they behead, rape, and murder in the name of Islam."
- "Jews, Christians and others are to be subdued so that Islam may 'prevail over all religions.'" It's all in the final chapter of the Quran: "Kill or be killed in battle, and paradise awaits…"
- A phenomenon of the last several years is the Muslim takeover of portions of cities around the world where non-Muslims are in danger of even passing through. The police are afraid to patrol the streets. Dearborn, MI is such a city. London, Paris and cities in Belgium and Sweden are prime examples. Can you think of a portion of a city anywhere in the world where a non-Christian is afraid to enter a Christian zone?

My God is a God of peace and love for our enemies. Scriptures abound. Here's just one: "You have heard that it was said, 'Love your neighbor and hate your enemy.' But I tell you, love your enemies and pray for those who persecute you, that you may be children of your Father in heaven. He causes his sun to rise on the evil and the good and sends rain on the righteous and the unrighteous." (Matthew 5:43-45)

In the interest of fairness, the gentleman I spoke with said, "Have you ever read the Old Testament? Does He sound like a God of peace there? Or, how about at the end of time as we know it (Revelation), where He destroys 1/3 of the earth's population?" Those are good, fair questions. It is that God is God, and He sets the rules. God was telling His people to eliminate terrorists and pagans who would mercilessly kill them, attempt to annihilate them or enslave them, and then have their women (the captors) seduce them away from Him into unholy bonds. The end of the Millennium marks the fulfillment of God's redemptive plan and the ultimate defeat of evil, leading to the establishment of God's eternal kingdom and the final judgment of all humanity. (Revelation 20:1-6) After the second coming of Christ, Satan is bound and cast into the bottomless pit, where he is confined for a thousand years on earth. During this time, Christ reigns in heaven with His saints, who are resurrected to life and reign with Him as priests, sharing in His authority and glory. At the end of the Millennium, Satan is released from his prison and marshals his forces to wage war against the saints and the beloved city that have descended from heaven. However, fire from heaven devours the enemies of God, and Satan is cast into the lake of fire and brimstone. This decisive victory over evil marks the culmination of God's redemptive plan and the final defeat of Satan and his allies.

Anyone who has a problem with God being God will not be satisfied with this answer.

E. GOD SPEAKS TO US THROUGH HIS WORD

Hebrews 1:1,2 says "In the past God spoke to our ancestors through the prophets at many times and in various ways, 2 but in these last days he has spoken to us by his Son, whom he appointed heir of all things, and through whom also he made the universe. How is that possible? Through His Word.

I Thessalonians 1:5 says: "…our gospel came to you not simply with words, but also in power, with the Holy Spirit, and deep conviction" and "For the appeal we make does not spring from error or impure motives, nor are we trying to trick you…" (2:3) In other words, God spoke to Paul, and then he recorded it as scripture.

Are you willing to believe what God says to you through His Word? A key Hebrew word for *to hear* is also translated as *to obey*! When God calls us to hear His voice, He is calling us not only to listen intelligently and attentively, but He is also saying, "Whoever has my commands and keeps them is the one who loves me. The one who loves me will be loved by my Father, and I too will love them and show myself to them." "Anyone who loves me will obey my teaching. My Father will love them, and we will come to them and make our home with them." (John 14:21,23) Love Him and know His word.

Chris Teigreen has several excellent thoughts: "Just as Jesus did and said many things that were never recorded in the gospels (John 21:25), God has many thoughts that have not been written in the Word. The Bible is the lens through which we see the realms of heaven and earth, and all that the Spirit says will be consistent with it. But He leads us into deep mysteries and shares His heart in personal ways. He directs our steps individually and opens our eyes to the ways God works in our lives."

F. THE WHOLE COUNCIL OF GOD

"Do your best to present yourself to God as one approved, a worker who does not need to be ashamed and who correctly handles the word of truth." (II Tim 2:15)

In Acts 20, Paul says goodbye to his beloved friends in Ephesus, knowing that he will never see them again. In verses 25-27, he says, "Now I know that none of you among whom I have gone about preaching the kingdom will ever see me again. Therefore, I declare to you today that I am innocent of the blood of any of you. For I have not hesitated to proclaim to you the whole will of God."

I want to raise an honest question to which I do not have a definitive answer: what is the whole counsel of God? Do not suppose that I am questioning any part of God's revealed word. I am asking who I should believe to be telling the whole counsel of God?

- the Calvinists or the Armenians?
- the traditionalists or the charismatics?
- the legalists, fundamentalists, conservatives or modernists?
- the topical preachers or the expositors?
- the premillennialists, postmillennialists, a-millennialists, etc.?
- the well-known TV preachers/evangelists/healers or the faithful pastors of normal congregations who have little to show for their faithful labors?
- the preachers/teachers who plumb the depths in every message verse by verse, book by book, or the preachers who address a topic and interpret it with scriptural support it with many practical illustrations?

It can be conscious-soothing to read a brief devotional every day. Reading through the Bible in a year can be impressive and commendable. But do you know what you read, can you remember it, and do you apply it? Or is it just an exercise in fulfilling what you have been told every good Christian should do?

Our theme verse in the King James reads, "Study to show thyself approved unto God… rightly dividing the word of truth." Study! Be ready to defend. I'm not sure God gives extra credit just for reading, though it certainly can't hurt, and it's better than not even cracking your Bible! And then apply, put what you have read into practice, and live it out. Reading it and setting it aside is not God's plan. Study!

You will never be able to accurately apply the word of God if you don't know what it says! Is studying, evaluating, and discerning a part of your daily routine? Only then can the Spirit guide you in all truth. He does not scribble nuggets on a blank spiritual slate!

"First, I shake the whole (apple) tree, that the ripest might fall. Then I climb the tree and shake each limb, and then each branch and then each twig, and then I look under each leaf!" - Martin Luther

G. BIBLE TRANSLATIONS

"For the Word that God speaks is alive and full of power [making it active, operative, energizing, and effective]; it is sharper than any two-edged sword, penetrating to the dividing line of the breath of life (soul) and [the immortal] spirit, and of joints and marrow [of the deepest parts of our nature], exposing *and* sifting *and* analyzing *and* judging the very thoughts and purposes of the heart." (Heb. 4:12) Amplified Bible

Some Christians wonder which Bible translation is "best." Well, that depends on a few factors. But the vital issue is not which translation is best, instead, do you read the translation(s) you have? They all can penetrate your mind and soul.

With the language changing rather rapidly today, it may be helpful to understand the following:

- The KJV (King James Version) and NASB (New American Standard Bible) attempted to take the underlying Hebrew and Greek words and translate them into the closest corresponding English words.

- The NIV (New International Version) and NLT (New Living Translation) attempted to take the underlying Hebrew and Greek thought and put it into the current English thought (thought for thought).
- Paraphrases such as the Living Bible or The Message attempt to present a different perspective on the meaning of the verse, which will be very understandable. These are not translations but rather the author's attempt to put the meaning in his own words.

For basic Bible study, it would be best to compare the KJV and NIV or the NASB and NLT to get a feel for what they say. It is essential to put the verse in context. Standing alone, you can prove almost anything you want! Having done this, go to TLB or The Message to get a feeling for the verse in today's vernacular.

I like to use the Amplified Bible, which gives you many nuances to the words used. (See the opening verse.)

The tool I find most helpful (and this is only one of many such websites) is Bible Gateway. com, which gives you all versions on one page, verse by verse. It also has a wonderful search tool to find the verse you seek. It is a tremendous resource and timesaver.

I have several friends who do quite a bit of scripture memorization and tell me that The King James is easiest to learn and remember over time. A ThD friend likes the HCSB (Holman Christian Standard Bible) best.

Do you want to know what a Bible text means? Put it in its context (which might include many verses), read it in four or five versions followed by one or two paraphrases, and you'll have a great understanding. (Or it may clarify some questions you have in mind so that you can research them better.) Those who know the Bible best love it most.

Here is an example of Psalm 23:1 in the above translations, showing you the difference. All of these and many more are available on Bible Gateway.

> KJV: "The Lord is my shepherd; I shall not want."
>
> NASB: "The Lord is my shepherd; I will not be in need."
>
> NIV: "The Lord is my shepherd, I lack nothing."
>
> NLT: "The Lord is my shepherd; I have all that I need."

HCSB: "The Lord is my shepherd; there is nothing I lack."

Amplified Bible: "The Lord is my Shepherd [to feed, to guide and to shield me], I shall not want."

The Message: "God, my shepherd! I don't need a thing."

TLB: "Because the Lord is my Shepherd, I have everything I need!"

One of my great joys in retirement, when I have a good amount of spare time, is to take a topic that interests me or that I don't fully understand and go to all the sources I mention to come up with a resolution. This is how many of my devotionals are formed. Then, I try to make them understandable and illustrate from my life and experiences with Christian leaders and what they have shared with me.

I encourage you to get into your Bible with whichever version(s) you choose. Is there a subject that interests you and you want to research? Type it in search on your home page and/or type in GotQuestions.org to get you started and well on your way. You will find this exhilarating.

H. ETERNAL SECURITY OR PERSEVERANCE OF THE SAINTS?

There are centuries-old debates in the Bible that have been discussed by theologians of great repute but who hold totally opposite points of view! These include faith vs. works, positions on eschatology, security of the believer vs. perseverance of the saints, etc. Once you receive Christ, are you secure forever, or does that belief need to be confirmed by living a life for Christ?

Who am I to think I am if these spiritual giants cannot resolve the problem(s)? Yet, ignorance is not bliss. I am commanded to "be prepared to give an answer to everyone who asks you to give the reason for the hope that you have (I Pet. 3:15) and to prayerfully and thoughtfully come to conclusions that satisfy my heart based on my understanding of the scriptures. God does not commend our buying thoughtlessly into the theology of any individual, no matter how revered that person may be.

Eugene Peterson lays out the debate in his book, "A Long Obedience in the Same Direction" (pages 85,86) that God will never let us go; we are eternally secure, but we can *purposely, willfully* reject him and he will not hold us back, he will grant our wish. Defection requires a *deliberate, sustained* act of rejection. In such cases, there is no chance of further repentance. "It is impossible for those who have once been enlightened, who have tasted the heavenly gift, who have shared in the Holy Spirit, who have tasted the goodness of the word of God and the powers of the coming age and who have fallen away, to be brought back to repentance. To their loss they are crucifying the Son of God all over again and subjecting him to public disgrace." (Hebrews 6:4-6) I have spoken with people who do not interpret those verses similarly, yet it seems clear to me.

We all have seen people receive the Lord, walk with Him for a certain period of time and then slowly slip away. There is no debate about this. This phenomenon is rampant today. The question probably is, were they ever saved in the first place? Only God knows.

After years of confusion and searching for my heart's satisfaction, I read Peterson's explanation, which I embrace. Based on much research, I have drawn my conclusions on Hebrews 6.

Today, I found two verses I had read many times but had not fully processed. In I Chron 28:9 &10, David instructs Solomon to build the temple.

I Chron. 28:9, 10: "And you, my son Solomon, acknowledge the God of your father, and serve him with wholehearted devotion and with a willing mind, for the Lord searches *every* heart and understands every desire and every thought. If you seek him, he will be found by you; but if you forsake him, he will *reject you forever*. Consider now, for the Lord has chosen you to build a house as the sanctuary. Be strong and do the work." It is accurate to note that David stated this directly to his son, Solomon, for a definite purpose. However, note my emphasized words: "every" and "reject you forever." That does not sound like it was meant for just one person at one particular time.

ROBERT KRAMER ON ETERNAL SECURITY VS. PERSEVERANCE OF THE SAINTS

Here is a study by Robert Kramer, a former pastor in the denomination where I was raised. Once he retired, he researched doctrines he held that were required by the denomination. Once he retired, he could state his findings. I have greatly abbreviated it, giving just the basics. I have not altered his thoughts in any way. I have not quoted all of the verses simply in the interest of space.

ULTIMATE SALVATION IS CONDITIONAL
UPON PRESENT TENSE FAITH

A. THE "IF" PASSAGES

These texts state that our ultimate salvation is secure "if" certain conditions are maintained.

- If One Abides in Jesus & His Word; John 8:31,32,51; John 15:1-14; I Cor.15:1,2
- If One Continues in God's Grace: Romans 11:21-23: Galatians 5:1-6
- If One Continues in the Faith and Does Not Move Away From the Gospel: Colossians 1:22-23
- If One Holds Fast Until the End: Hebrews3:6,12,14
- If One's Lifestyle Reflects Fellowship with Christ: I John 1:6-7

We have presented texts that clearly affirm that our ultimate salvation is conditional. There are additional passages that may not state the case as clearly as those above, but when properly understood, they also teach the necessity of continuing faith and obedience for one to remain a Christian. Some use the word "if," while others state a condition necessary for salvation without the exact wording. Those passages are Matthew 5:13; 18:21-35, Luke 12:42-48, Acts 5:32, Romans 6:15-23, II Timothy 2:11-13, Hebrews 10:38-39,1 Peter 1:5-13, I John 2:15-17, II John 1:9, Revelation 3:5 and 20:15.

B. ULTIMATE SALVATION IS ASSURED IF
ONE DOES NOT FALL AWAY

These texts clearly teach the possibility of departing from a faith and relationship once held.

- Falling Away from the Saving Word: Mark 4:6, Luke 8:6 lit. (dried up), Matt. 13:20)
- Falling Away from the Faith; Jude 3 tied with I Tim 4:1
- Falling Away from Grace: Gal. 5:1,4
- Falling Away from the Living God; Hebrews 3:12

ADDITIONAL FALLING AWAY PASSAGES

Additional Scriptural texts express the idea of falling away but use other terms to express it. In John 6:66-71 some <u>WITHDREW</u> from following Christ; in I Timothy 5:8, some <u>DENIED</u> the faith by their lifestyle; in II Peter 2:18-22 some *"after they have escaped the defilements of the world by the knowledge (personal experience) of the Lord and Savior Jesus Christ, they are <u>AGAIN ENTANGLED</u> in them and are <u>overcome</u>...;"* in I Timothy 6:20-21 some have *"<u>GONE ASTRAY</u> from the faith"* by yielding to *"worldly and empty chatter...and what is falsely called knowledge;"* in James 5:19-20 some *"<u>STRAY</u> from the truth"* into *"the error of his way;"* in Romans 11:20-22 some Jews *"FELL* into unbelief and were broken off of the olive tree of grace; and in Galatians 1:6 some *"<u>DESERTED</u> "* Christ for a different gospel. (KJB)

So I have a part—a responsibility to respond, hence the first step of life-saving belief. And beyond that, I have the responsibility of remaining faithful to the end, exerting my free will to love God with all my heart, shown by obedience (John 14:21), and staying in continuous fellowship with Him. The balance of grace and works appears to be a holy tension that cannot be separated. While He will not leave me or go back on His covenant with me (if we are faithless, he will remain faithful—2 Timothy 2:13), it appears that I can choose to end my agreement with Him (if we endure, we will also reign with him. If we disown him, he will also disown us—vs. 2:12). (KJB)

I. PARDON

A pardon is a government decision to relieve a person of some or all of the legal consequences of a criminal conviction. Pardons are sometimes offered to persons who were wrongfully convicted or claim to have been wrongfully convicted.

The cycle of years has reached the point that once a President is about to leave power, he exercises some of his final authority in pardoning anyone for any reason he wishes. Every cycle is the same; that is, every president has pardoned persons who many people think do not deserve it or who many feel it is a "thank you" for personal assistance that may have been illegal and for which they have been convicted and sentenced. Barack Obama granted clemency 1,927 times during his eight years in office. Donald Trump, by comparison, has used it only 45 times, though he is expected to make many more before leaving office. The controversy is always over who and why a person has been pardoned. Gerald Ford pardoned Richard Nixon, George H.W. Bush pardoned Casper Weinberger, and Bill Clinton pardoned Marc Rich. All were guilty!

Writing in 1833 about the President's clemency power, Chief Justice John Marshall said, "It will always entail an act of grace, proceeding from the power entrusted with the execution of the laws." Since no set of laws can be specific enough for all the occasions which warrant grace and mercy, its proper use depends on the judgment and propriety of those who wield it.

Presumably, all who have been pardoned over the years are grateful. That's emotion. What about the following actions? Do those pardoned return to their old ways or show their gratitude through a new lifestyle?

Note the beginning words of the following verse: "Let the wicked forsake his way, and the unrighteous man his thoughts: and let him return unto the Lord, and he will have mercy upon him; and to our God, for he will abundantly pardon." (Isaiah 55:7)

For the sake of your name, Lord, forgive my iniquity, though it is great." (Psalm 25:11) David received that pardon, repented and went on to be a man after God's own heart.

Of particular note is that the word pardon is never used in the New Testament. Instead, three words are used to clearly state that our sins are forgiven (pardoned). Louw and Nida say "aphiemi," "aphesis" and "apoluo" all mean "to remove the guilt resulting from wrongdoing…It is extremely important to note that *the focus in the meanings* of 'aphiemi,' 'aphesis' and 'apoluo' is upon the guilt of the wrongdoer and not upon the wrongdoing itself. *When God forgives the wrongdoer, the event of wrongdoing is not undone, but the guilt resulting from such an event is pardoned.* To forgive, therefore, means essentially to remove the guilt resulting from wrongdoing." (Emphasis mine.)

Thank God that the Supreme Commander-in-Chief, the King of Kings, issued my pardon, my forgiveness of sins. The difference between God's pardon and man's is that God forgets, and man doesn't. Man keeps records; God wipes out records. Now, my part of the bargain is to walk in the newness of life out of a debt of gratitude.

"Pardon for sin and a peace that endureth,
Thine own dear presence to cheer and to guide.
Strength for today and bright hope for tomorrow,
Blessings all mine with ten thousand beside.
Great is thy faithfulness…" –Thomas Chisholm

"Grace, grace, God's grace,
Grace that will pardon and cleanse my sin." –Julia H. Johnston

I sincerely trust that you have spent enough time reading and studying this chapter to speak intelligently about it with others who may have questions.

CHAPTER

2

LEGALISM

LEGALISM AND LIBERTY DEFINED

"Often, legalism is identified by rules: do this; don't do that. But it is not. Legalism is not the law. Legalism is an attitude. Legalism exists when you conform to a rule or code with the motivation of exalting yourself. So, the law does not make you a legalist. However, the attitude in which you apply the law could very quickly give you the badge.

"Liberty is freedom. The question is, are there limits? We celebrate our freedom in the US, but that doesn't mean we can do anything we want. There are limits and laws! As believers, our liberty is limited by our love for each other…in that we choose not to exercise our freedom if we know it could cause another believer to struggle in his/her spiritual life. My love for them limits my liberty."—Paul Nyquist

A. THE POSITIVES AND NEGATIVES OF LEGALISM

I was raised in a very legalist church, went to a legalistic college, traveled with a legalist evangelist, directed choirs in legalistic churches, worked in several legalist ministries, etc. Does it surprise you that my first reaction to any lifestyle issue is legalistic? We were taught that we had the spiritual gift of discernment, being translated as criticism!

I escaped that system that controlled me. I had to until the day I retired. …I was on their payroll. After retirement, I decided to think for myself by studying passages that confused me, observing other Christians who did not believe as I (they) believed, and remembering the gross inconsistencies of those who defined outwardly what an honest Christian is.

I received a note from a dear friend the other day that asked, " Were those days all bad?" I thought I had made it clear several times that they weren't, but now I want to reiterate that.

If you get bored in the middle for some reason, don't forget, there were many good things from those days. I want to unwrap that.

Let's clarify from the beginning that this never had to do with essential doctrine. I have always believed in the inerrancy of scripture, the virgin birth, the Trinity, the doctrine of the new birth, heaven, and hell, and a Christian lifestyle to substantiate the new life in Christ. I was, and still am, a fundamentalist, which means that I believe in all of the fundamentals the Bible teaches. However, traditional fundamentalists add all the trappings of legalism. That's where I bail out.

But that's where we butt heads. What the legalists say about the Christian walk and what the Bible says are different. The Pharisees (legalists in Jesus' days) tried to follow the 613 commandments of the Mosaic Law, and thousands of new commandments were created to clarify the original 613 commandments. The legalists of today have their own definitions of issues, as did the Pharisees. The layers go on and on.

To begin to unwrap this isn't easy because, in contemporary society, the norms have gone from the North Pole to the South Pole. There is no moderate zone.

I don't want to bore you with details, but I want you to understand clearly. Some of this should bring more than a chuckle.

Let's list some of the restrictions. They all have a nugget of truth, but complete denial of any is unrealistic. This is how I lived.

1. Smoking: your body is the temple of the Holy Spirit, and you should not defile it.
2. Alcoholic beverages: all alcohol is sinful. It makes you lose control of your senses and do things you would otherwise not do.
3. Dancing: It is sensual and stirs feelings inside, from body to body. Dances lead to what happens next following the dance.

4. Modesty:
   a. Women had to have long hair, and men had short hair. Beards were not good on men. In my senior year of college, the administration brought in a medical doctor and his wife to talk to the student body about sex. The man went with the man and the woman with his wife. It was almost funny. They must have thought we just crawled out from under a toadstool or something. The only thing I remember is that beards were not good for men because they represented the private parts of a woman! I didn't know that.
   b. Tight clothing revealing body lines was taboo.
   c. Women had to wear skirts or dresses, no pants; men had to wear trousers. Our son was in a growth stage and could not wear bell-bottom trousers because they represented the world. We had to purchase trousers for him, and my wife had to adjust them to take out the bell bottoms! On the women in pants issue, one of my friends with a doctorate in theology was passing a church on a Sunday morning and decided to stop. When they went to enter, an usher stopped them and said they could not come in because his wife had on a pantsuit.
   d. Women had to wear modest one-piece bathing suits, and men had to wear tee shirts. Some groups did not even permit mixed bathing.
   e. Makeup was frowned upon unless it was almost unnoticeable. Two unsaved girls wearing heavy makeup went to church with a girlfriend. (They didn't know any better.) The pastor's wife stood at the door and made them take off their makeup before she admitted them.
   f. Playing cards: they were the devil's tools. They led to gambling. Playing other card games with other decks was permissible!
   g. Movies. Never. We couldn't even go to the theater to see a Billy Graham movie, apparently because even the building was of the devil.
   h. TV. We were not allowed to have a TV in our house until I was on Percy Crawford's coast-to-coast TV program (evangelistic), and then it was OK to watch. Our pastor at the time had 7 children, and for years, he did not allow a TV in the house, so the kids went to their friends' houses to watch TV.
   i. Purchasing anything on Sunday. No shopping, even for groceries. But you could go to eat at a restaurant. At our Bible conference, Sunday was the most financially active day of the week, with the purchase of meals for day guests and the check-ins for the new week. Go figure!
   j. No sports or any activities on Sunday. You attend church, Sunday School, Youth Group, and the evening service. Sleep in the afternoon!

k. In my day, any music with a beat was sinful. (I know all music has a beat, but you probably know what I mean!) The devil was in all syncopation. Many instruments were unacceptable, especially the drums and the bass guitar! And on it goes. Today, everything is acceptable, and the louder and more rhythmic, the better. And be sure to add lighting and smoke.

Please don't make the mistake of assuming I am sighting unusual cases. Trust me, I could write a book just on my own experiences. If you think these examples are out of the ordinary, you are in denial.

After being in the Bible Conference ministry for 40 years, I could recount the names, dates, issues, etc., of gross inconsistencies in the guest speakers and musicians. One nationally known radio pastor was the most miserable Christian I ever met.

How much more evidence do you need? I could do as some, blame my failures on others, but that would only be deceiving myself. Some of the people I've seen crash and burn stagger me. How true that man will let you down, including my potential for the same.

Legalism did not harm me, but it damaged me to some extent. It had some very strong points.

B. THE FALLOUT FROM LEGALISM

One more thing must be said because some of you may not be well-versed in scripture, and I cannot make any assumptions. Legalism, as I am using it in this document, was practiced by a segment of the Jewish society who thought themselves more spiritual than all others. There were so many rules that they couldn't remember them all. Thus, it is with modern-day Pharisees, the legalists I am referring to.

Before I get into details, *let me state clearly that legalism was not all bad*. There clearly are rules, regulations, expectations in scripture. Legalism is one extreme and permissiveness (as in today's Christian society) is the other. Both are tools of the devil! All of those rules kept me out of a lot of trouble as a teenager. Unfortunately, it also drove thousands in the opposite direction.

But that is not the point. What is the result of all of those restrictions?

Do you remember when Proverbs 23:6 was the law of the land— "Start children off on the way they should go, and even when they are old they will not turn from it.." And what are the results? Ask missionaries, evangelists, preachers, Christian workers, etc. The defection rate is alarming. In Matthew 23:4 we read, "They tie up heavy, cumbersome loads and put them on other people's shoulders, but they themselves are not willing to lift a finger to move them." This refers to the Pharisees with all of their man-made laws (613). But they themselves will not follow their own laws. In the 1970s at the Bible conference where I served, I made it a point to ask every speaker who the modern Pharisees are. Almost all said the fundamentalists. I know, and you know, dozens of people who want nothing to do with the church or the Bible today because they were burned as young people. Perhaps you have experienced this in your own household or close circle of friends. They saw too much hypocrisy, even in their own households. Now that I am out of my spiritual bubble, I run into this time and time again. People who know the way, know the right things to do and reject it because they were turned off by what they saw as reality in too many lives.

My Bible says that Jesus came so that our joy might be made full. (I John 1:4; John 16:24) It also says, "Come to me, all you who are weary and burdened, and I will give you rest. Take my yoke upon you and learn from me, for I am gentle and humble in heart, and you will find rest for your souls." (Matt. 11:28,29) The fundamentalist version of that is, "Come unto me all ye that labor and are heavy laden and I will give you laws to follow so that you may be approved, and you will not find rest until you do!"

For emphasis, I want to state again that this was okay for some people like me. I weathered the storm. It grieves me, however, as I speak with so many people who just plain deserted. I grieve also at the laxity of today's society. There needs to be balance.

C. NOT A BAD DEAL

Those who know me may have heard me refer to my legalistic roots and associations. I have [in recent years] spelled out to some degree how I feel I have matured spiritually since I retired, while my legalistic friends would say I digressed. I no longer think God is pleased primarily with what I do not do but instead with what I do. The new challenge is, do I do what I am supposed to do?

I no longer feel shackled by all the "don'ts" in my life, although I still refrain from certain practices when with friends who I believe may be offended by them.

In high school, college, and my entire "professional" life in the ministry, I lived in a glass house, and people were always watching my every move and quite often throwing stones. It was (and is) impossible to live up to all expectations. While I understand that the standard of the laws of God is impossible, thus the need for salvation and grace, I always felt I could not even keep the laws of "the church." Further, they kept changing depending on the people involved, the time, and the place. The rules were not the same in Pennsylvania as New York, Michigan as in Maryland, or New England as in Florida.

But looking back, all of those rules were never a really bad deal. Think about it this way:

- I never had to be worried about any complications related to drunkenness (car accidents, fights, etc.)
- I never had to worry about being caught carrying or using drugs
- I never had to worry that my wife would find out about an affair or that some woman's husband would come and shoot me
- I never had to worry that my sin would eventually catch up with me or that I would be exposed and disgrace my family
- I never had to worry that I would contract one of the physical problems usually
- associated with a worldly lifestyle (sexually transmitted disease, lung cancer, sclerosis of the liver, etc.)
- I never had to worry that the police would show up at my door someday and arrest me for thievery, disturbing the peace, molestation, or any similar offense.

The list could go on, but you get the point. That's not a bad deal at all!

I now quickly add that I never was an angel and still haven't sprouted wings. As I have said before, if you knew everything about me (right up to this present day), you probably would never want to read this book. The point is not how good I am; instead, it is how hindsight has made me realize that all the past legalistic restrictions under which I lived really didn't hurt me and probably helped me. They may have been overkill, but they also sheltered me.

And all that causes me to wonder if there are too few restrictions on Christians today. Is it because I came from so many rules that they seem "normal," or is life without rules freedom? What is freedom? Does it mean you can do whatever you choose anytime, under any circumstances? Obviously not. One dictionary definition is this: the quality of the will of the life of the individual of *not being totally constrained*; able to *choose between alternative activities* in identical circumstances. *Note the qualifiers in italics.*

Need I go on?

In Galatians 5:1,13-15 we read, "Come to me, all you who are weary and burdened, and I will give you rest. Take my yoke upon you and learn from me, for I am gentle and humble in heart, and you will find rest for your souls....."You, my brothers and sisters, were called to be free. But do not use your freedom to indulge the flesh; rather, serve one another humbly in love" For the entire law is fulfilled in keeping this one command: "Love your neighbor as yourself.' If you bite and devour each other, watch out or you will be destroyed by each other."

If (Jewish and) current legalists take the law, a good thing, and add their additional restrictions, are we today in current Christianity taking that same good law and re-interpreting it with our exceptions according to our own desires? Is the old way terrible and the new way good, just by definition? Should the church remain static, unchanging, old-fashioned? Absolutely not. Change is inevitable. Many churches are dying because they refuse to change. But how much and what change is necessary so that contemporary is not simply a mirror of the world with a cross displayed on the wall?

In this day, how do we interpret, "For everything in the world—the lust of the flesh, the lust of the eyes, and the pride of life—comes not from the Father but from the world.." (I John 2:16) Are some defined standards (as opposed to none) being "critical and catty," "ruining each other"?

The laws of God are not a bad deal. Try living without them. If you don't know where to start, how about the Ten Suggestions? (Oops, that was Commandments.) Can you imagine what life would be without civil laws? It's called anarchy. Are we on the verge of spiritual anarchy? Is what we like, what pleases us, more important than what pleases God?

I ask the questions, and you fill in the blanks. Think about it; don't just read it and forget it.

D. RECOVERING LEGALIST

I no longer subscribe to all of the rules and regulations under which I grew up and served in ministry for 25 years.

I was talking with a woman who had been a nun and taught Catholic school for many years. We talked about people wearing masks while all alone, walking, bicycling, kayaking, or in a car. Alone! (This was during Covid.) Then she made a brilliant statement: "Some people have lived under strict rules for so long, they don't know how to live outside of them, and actually feel more comfortable living under rules made by others who they consider wiser." Forget that statistics show that fresh air is good for you. I'm sure many come from the same essential background as I do.

It is this thinking I now reject.

I wish to present a series of verses, with a few comments, that will validate why I was wrong. Fasten your seatbelt.

1. The entire word of God is authoritative.

    II Timothy 3: 16-17 "All Scripture is God-breathed and is useful for teaching, rebuking, correcting and training in righteousness, so that the servant of God may be thoroughly equipped for every good work." You cannot pick and choose. You cannot overlook teaching verses because they do not fit your narrative.

2. We are no longer under the law in the New Covenant.

    a. Jesus came to fulfill the law. "Do not think that I have come to abolish the Law or the Prophets; I have not come to abolish them but to fulfill them.." Matthew 5:17 "For he himself is our peace, who has made the two groups one and has destroyed the barrier, the dividing wall of hostility, by setting aside in his flesh the law with its commands and regulations. His purpose was to create in himself one new humanity out of the two, thus making peace, and in one body to reconcile both of them to God through the cross, by which he put to death their hostility." Ephesians 2:14-16

b. In the Old Covenant, the Jews had 600 commandments, 350 items, and actions from which to abstain, and 250 were on the Jewish "to-do list." If you think we are still under the law, hear this: Galatians 3:2,3: "I would like to learn just one thing from you: Did you receive the Spirit by the works of the law, or by believing what you heard? Are you so foolish? After beginning by means of the Spirit, are you now trying to finish by means of the flesh (keeping the law)?"

Galatians 3:19, 21: "Is the law, therefore, opposed to the promises of God? Absolutely not! For if a law had been given that could impart life, then righteousness would certainly have come by the law." But the law could not save you.

c. You do not want to be under the law!

James 2:10, "For whoever keeps the whole law and yet stumbles at just one point is guilty of breaking all of it."

Galatians 3:10, "For all who rely on the works of the law are under a curse, as it is written: 'Cursed is everyone who does not continue to do everything written in the Book of the Law.'"

That means you cannot eat pork or shellfish, wear clothing with a mix of materials, do any work of any kind on the Sabbath, and you must tithe. Mess up with ONE of them and you are guilty of all. At our church, many years ago, an evangelist, Brother Bud, came for a week. One night he was expounding from an O.T. passage which says women should not wear men's clothes and noted that his wife wears a nightgown to bed "as women should," and not pajamas which are for men (pants).

Colossians 2:20 "Since you died with Christ to the elemental spiritual forces of this world, why, as though you still belonged to the world, do you submit to its rules: 'Do not handle! Do not taste! Do not touch!'? These rules, which have to do with things that are all destined to perish with use, are based on merely human commands and teachings. Regulations like this have an appearance of wisdom, with their self-imposed worship, their false humility and their harsh treatment of the body, but they lack any value in restraining sensual involvement."

3. If all of this is true, why do we bother at all with the Old Testament? Romans 7:5-8 "For when we were in the realm of the flesh, the sinful passions aroused by the law were at work in us, so that we bore fruit for death. But now, by dying to what once bound us, we have been released from the law so that we serve in the new way of the Spirit, and not in the old way of the written code. What shall we say, then? Is the law sinful? Certainly not! Nevertheless, I would not have known what sin was had it not been for the law. For I would not have known what coveting really was if the law had not said, 'You shall not covet.' But sin, seizing the opportunity afforded by the commandment, produced in me every kind of coveting. For apart from the law, sin was dead."

4. So, are there no rules?

   a. Please notice who the law is made for. I Timothy 1:8-11, "We know that the law is good if one uses it properly. We also know that the law is made not for the righteous but for lawbreakers and rebels, the ungodly and sinful, the unholy and irreligious, for those who kill their fathers or mothers, for murderers, for the sexually immoral, for those practicing homosexuality, for slave traders and liars and perjurers—and for whatever else is contrary to the sound doctrine that conforms to the gospel concerning the glory of the blessed God, which he entrusted to me."

   b. Paul gives guidance to proper Christian conduct. Ephesians 4:32 is a good place to begin: "Be kind and compassionate to one another, forgiving each other, just as in God through Christ forgave you." Philippians 4:8,9: "Finally, brothers and sisters, whatever is true, whatever is noble, whatever is right, whatever is pure, whatever is lovely, whatever is admirable—if anything is excellent or praiseworthy—think about such things. Whatever you have learned or received or heard from me, or seen in me—put it into practice. And the God of peace will be with you."

   c. "What you have learned and received and heard and seen in me—practice these things, and the God of peace will be with you." Galatians 5:22,23 "But the fruit of the Spirit is love, joy, peace, forbearance, kindness, goodness, faithfulness, gentleness and self-control. Against such things there is no law."

Are you beginning to understand the laws we were taught that made us "spiritual?" Do you see why I am a bit rebellious against legalists? Let's try the path of love. "Do to others as you would have them do to you." (Luke 6:31). Let's refrain from things we feel free to do based on our own convictions because we love other brothers and sisters in Christ and do not want to offend them, not because they are "wrong." "It is better not to eat meat or drink wine or to do anything else that will cause your brother or sister to fall." Romans 14:21

Skip all the non-scriptural rules…no clear teaching, no rule. I don't care about your interpretation.

Think about these things.

I offer several more examples of what I feel was foolishness.

The older generation than mine was highly legalistic, and that is the generation under which I served willingly. I love these ministries to this very moment. And they no longer operate as I now describe.

Sunday was the turnover day for the old crowd to leave and the new crowd to arrive during the summer conference season. As you would assume, they paid upon arrival. It also was the day of substantial drive-in guests to hear the well-known speaker of the week in the Sunday morning service. Thus, we sold dinner tickets to the drive-in crowd for the famous turkey dinner. We usually fed about 500. Obviously, they paid for the tickets.

Sunday was the day more money was exchanged than any other day of the week.

During the evening service, it was announced that "the snack shop will be open this evening following the meeting, but not to its full extent because we want to be a good testimony to our neighbors." What does "its full extent" mean? The grill was not open for hamburgers. Everything else was the same. Using logic, it was acceptable for all the other money spent on Sunday, but purchasing a hamburger in the evening was unacceptable because of our testimony to the neighbors. First, we had no neighbors with a vision of the property without a helicopter! Second, how could they see outside that helicopter that the grill was not open? Third, if the grill was unacceptable on Sunday, why was it acceptable the rest of the week? Fourth, would the neighbors care?

At another conference, Saturday was the arrival day, and busloads of teens would arrive for the week. By the time they settled in, it was dinner time. In the evening there was a required concert. The lake, the main attraction, was closed on Sunday, as were all other activities. The groups would load the kids on the bus and take them to a nearby beach for which there was a fee. There were meetings on Monday morning, and finally, activities and the lake were available on Monday afternoon. By this time, they had been on the grounds for about 48 hours.

As the new director, at my first board meeting following the summer season, I was asked, "Now that you have been here for the summer, what recommendations would you make?" My first was that I would open the lake on Sunday afternoon for the reasons stated above.

You must understand that most board members owned cottages on the lake and came for the weekend. Naturally, they wanted to use their boats and swim in the lake on Sunday. Some even invited speakers or musicians of the week to join them.

Two board members stated that if we opened the lake, they would resign from the board (neither had a place on the lake nor a boat). My response was this, "If all of you agree not to use the lake on Sunday, I will withdraw the suggestion."

They opened the lake, and the two board members resigned!

E. TRADITIONS YOU CAN TRUST

"So then, brothers, stand firm and hold to the traditions that you were taught by us, either by our spoken word or by our letter." (2 Thessalonians 2:15, ESV). Focus on the word "traditions."

How does that strike you? Holding onto "traditions." Standing firm on "traditions." Traditions are legalistic; they are not from the Bible but from practices and concepts from the past, which we hold dear.

The Bible routinely condemns tradition whenever it's held as an authority over Scripture. Jesus told the scribes and Pharisees, "You nullify the word of God for the sake of your tradition." (Matthew 15:6) Paul warned the early church to "Why, then, was the law given at all? It was added because of transgressions until the Seed to whom the promise referred had come. The law was given through angels and entrusted to a mediator. A mediator, however, implies more than one party; but God is one. Is the law, therefore, opposed to the promises of God? Absolutely not! For if a law had been given that could impart life, then righteousness would certainly have come by the law." (Gal. 3: 19-21). Make your own list of religious things Christians do and believe that are not in the Bible. The examples are many and insidious. Wastes of time, if not wholly misguided.

So, when Paul told the Thessalonian believers to "stand firm and hold to the traditions" that he and other faithful ministers had spoken and written about to them, he wasn't talking at all about unhelpful, unholy traditions—what we might perceive as the "traditional" sense of that word. He spoke of things found in the Bible, things God had said, affirmed, and inspired by His Spirit. True things. Things that could be trusted.

I recently cataloged a list of biblical truths I've taught so often in our church that I'm sure people who've heard me say them can about hear them in their sleep. These themes include things like:

- If you're wrong in the way you're right, you're wrong even if you're right.
- God's love is not a pampering love but perfecting love.
- There are no enduring relationships without forgiveness.
- Gratitude is the attitude that sets the altitude for living.
- Choose to sin; choose to suffer.
- (And its flipside): Every time God says "Don't," He means, "Don't hurt yourself."

Are those just rote "traditions" to pass along? No. Statements like these are truths from the Word of Truth. They're the things I need engraved on my heart. They're the things to which we can "stand firm" and "hold" because they're what God teaches us in the Bible.

Do you have them? These kinds of "traditions"? And are you reading, studying, hearing, teaching, and doing them? Living them? Letting them change you?

Hold fast to what the Lord has revealed to you in His Word. Cling to those things when you're under pressure and feeling carried downstream by the rapids of life. Stand firm. Grab on. "Be strong in the Lord and the strength of his might" (Ephesians 6:11, ESV). "…continue in the faith, stable and steadfast, not shifting from the hope of the gospel that you heard" (Colossians 1:23). (ESV) "My brothers, whom I love and long for, my joy and crown, stand firm thus in the Lord, my beloved" (Philippians 4:1). (ESV) As Jesus asked of the Father for His disciples, "Sanctify them by your truth; your word is truth" (John 17:17). (ESV)

And as He does, "may our Lord Jesus Christ himself, and God our Father, who loved us and gave us eternal comfort and good hope through grace, comfort your hearts and establish them in every good work and word" (2 Thessalonians 2:16–17). (ESV)

F. BE A SPIRITUAL DETECTIVE

I want you to think with me, leaving as much emotion out of the equation as possible and accepting facts when they seem obvious, even though they may be contrary to what you have believed for a long time.

I have documented that I came from a very legalistic framework for over 50 years. The older and more aware I became of options other than those in my bubble, the more I questioned the validity of our narrow theology.

I have always had questions about the theology I was being "fed," but I reasoned that these people were more competent in the scriptures than I am and essentially accepted it.

But the first time I remember being upset by an issue, not just disagreeing, had to do with charismatics and speaking in tongues. (To clarify, I am not charismatic and do not speak in tongues, so I am not defending myself.) This occurred at least 50 years ago when the charismatics first became highly visible. A missionary from South America, supported by our church, gave a report that included mass revivals in charismatic circles in his South American, heavily Catholic country. He boldly stated that this was a work of the devil parading as an angel of light. I was furious. I remembered Matthew 12:31: "Why, then, was the law given at all? It was added because of transgressions until the Seed to whom the promise referred had come. The law was given through angels and entrusted to a mediator. A mediator, however, implies more than one party; but God is one. Is the law, therefore, opposed to the promises of God? Absolutely not! For if a law had been given that could impart life, then righteousness would certainly have come by the law." (Gal. 3:19-21 Since the Holy Spirit is involved in the process of salvation, is this blasphemy against Him? "Salvation is purposed by the Father, accomplished by the Son, and applied by the Holy Spirit. Without the Spirit's agency in salvation, all that Christ has accomplished brings no value to us. As Scripture uniformly presents, the Spirit graciously, effectively, and permanently gives us Christ Jesus and every blessing he has secured. Our salvation is in Christ alone. Our salvation is by his Spirit alone." David Garner

Speaking in tongues, divine healing, the baptism of the spirit, and the casting out of demons (in fact, I'm not sure we believe people in America could be demon-possessed!) were all explained away as evidence of the Christian experience just for Biblical times because there were no New Testament teachings yet written. Since we have complete revelation, these signs are no longer necessary. They would go on to say, and still do today, that these things happen in primitive societies where they have no Bible for the same reasons (confirmation).

Yet I hear from respectable, sensible Christians that these things are indeed happening here in the USA and other places around the world. Are they wrong, or is their theology incorrect? I could argue that as advanced as we are, we may be more ignorant of the actual teaching of the Bible than primitive societies, but we call it "progress" as we explain away what seems obvious.

Why are these signs and wonders prevalent where no theology is to be contradicted because they have none with their unadorned faith? Do these things happen only to babes in Christ who don't know any better, or have we become so theological that we limit the Lord?

You would be astounded at what he witnessed if you knew my son-in-law. He led a co-worker to Christ, yet that young man consistently had bizarre things happen to him. As a Christian, he knew instinctively they were not acceptable, but he seemed to have no power to overcome. His strange behavior was symptomatic of demon possession to a person who believes in such. Thus, the pastor asked my son-in-law to invite the man to his house to test for demon possession. His first thought was, "You've got to be kidding me." To cut to the chase, after several hours of discussion and prayer, the pastor began casting out the demon. There was convulsing, weird voices, thrashing, and total mayhem as one demon left, and there were more with the same actions. In relating the story, my son-in-law consistently reported his astonishment that this could be happening because it didn't fit his theology. It didn't fit mine, either, but it happened in Massachusetts, not Mozambique. The young man was (and is) a highly educated, skilled technical specialist and strong Christian today.

My daughter was one of four women who prayed over her working colleague who showed signs of demon possession. She was scared out of her wits. The woman doing most of the talking was an experienced counselor, and while praying, she addressed the demons and cast them out. (There was no weird scene as in the above story.) A short time later, the colleague came to my daughter and confessed that she was on the verge of having a sexual relationship with a male colleague. My daughter spoke with her and counseled, quoting many verses. The woman seemed in a trance, leaning to one side and looking down. The next day, the woman told her that while she was quoting verses, a demon was screaming in her other ear, and she was watching him fall into an abyss. This woman knew nothing about the Bible and didn't even know there was a bottomless pit called the Abyss. (Luke 8:21 and Revelation 9:1)

My granddaughter, serving as a missionary in Zambia, went from village to village, witnessing door-to-door in huts. She saw many conversions and actual healings explainable as nothing but that. One of many things happened with her team. Even in the early morning, a bar was open and filled with customers, so the team asked the owner if they could tell people about Jesus. After doing so, most patrons wanted to become Christians. Two lines were formed for individual prayer. Several were baptized with the Holy Spirit and healed on the spot. In another village, she was challenged by a man who said, "If your Jesus is so great, ask Him to heal my ankle. I've never walked normally." This was out of her comfort zone! But she prayed and, while doing so, was holding his ankle. She felt something happening. When she stopped praying, the man got up and walked normally. That doesn't fit my theology. She didn't believe in this "weird stuff" either until she experienced it first-hand.

I have never witnessed a divine (faith) healing. I have been a part of groups that have laid on hands and prayed for healing, and I have known people who have prayed for it for their loved ones, etc. I have no reason to believe. But my son-in-law, born into a military family serving in Japan at the time, tells me he was perhaps five years old, and his tear ducts did not function. Every morning, they had to put compresses on his eyes so that he could open them. His great-great-grandmother was a prayer warrior and called her "group" together here in the US the night before his surgery in Japan. The following day, he was in the hospital, prepared for surgery, and taken into the operating room and the doctors said there was no need for surgery and sent him home. Can I not believe him?

I am increasingly convinced that my theology is faulty. What I was taught is America's version of the gospel. I am also increasingly confident that we were wrong about many things. We often don't believe the Bible; we believe what we have been told about it and read and study it through those lenses.

This would make sense if we read what the Bible says in the Book of Acts and believed it as the Pentecostals did.

Is it time I allow God to be God and allow Him to do as He wishes, whether I believe it or not? "Why, then, was the law given at all? It was added because of transgressions until the Seed to whom the promise referred had come. The law was given through angels and entrusted to a mediator. A mediator, however, implies more than one party; but God is one. Is the law, therefore, opposed to the promises of God? Absolutely not! For if a law had been given that could impart life, then righteousness would certainly have come by the law." (Gal. 3:19-21)

Was this only for "that day?" I am fully aware of Matthew 24:24 and Mark 13:22, which warn us that in the end times (whenever and however long they are), false prophets will arise and show great signs and wonders to possibly even deceive the elect. But I am also aware of Luke 11:18, which says, "Acts 2:43:." Will Satan or a demon preach Jesus? We are not talking about preaching and teaching *false doctrine*; we are teaching *precisely what the Bible says rather than what we want it to say.*

I know there are severe abuses on the Pentecostal side. Are there just as many abuses in the exact reverse by the "frozen chosen" with little or no emotion or the all-knowing fundamentalists who have definitive, inspired answers for questions that have never even been asked?

Check this from the NIV: "But there were also false prophets among the people, just as there will be false teachers among you. They will secretly introduce destructive heresies, even denying the sovereign Lord who bought them—bringing swift destruction on themselves." (II Peter 2:1)

In sports, replays give different angles to a specific play. Let's try that. Recognizing the above verses dealing with false prophets (teachers) and the fact that a messenger of Satan would not teach the truth about Jesus, will another angle yield better information? Suppose the false teacher is a born-again believer teaching a poor, personal interpretation of what a passage(s) in the Bible means. Could that deceive even the elect? We do have our "Protestant Popes," you know! They may not deny the Lord, but they could teach false doctrine (interpretation) that contradicts God's meaning.

If there is a conclusion to this, I would state it as such: I have to ask myself if I am ready to accept what the Bible says, or will I doggedly hang on to what man says about what God says?

How about you? Are you willing to be a spiritual detective and examine the raw facts, or will you be satisfied with what others think they have discovered? I sincerely advise you to carefully consider what I have presented and not simply accept or reject it. Remember my purpose, to make you think, and my core verse, "Study to show yourselves approved..."

G. PLANNED OBEDIENCE

These days, we are hearing far too frequently about people who plan violence—school and nightclub shootings, violent workplace activity, attacks on political individuals, etc. People get angry and upset and begin to plan revenge and retaliation.

What would happen if Christians got so in love with the Lord that they planned obedience. Mostly, it would be reasonably easy to plan but far more challenging to execute.

The Bible speaks so clearly on many issues that individuals interpret with their own bias to support their desires. What was once black and white has turned to all shades of gray. And look at the results: a Christian society that can no longer be distinguished from a secular society.

Yes, some legalists added rules to the Biblical set of laws. No, certain things that were verboten will not send you to hell. On the other hand, if you claim to be a Christian and continue in what is a sin, you had better rethink what you thought receiving Christ was all about.

These verses highlight what has been considered sin from the earliest Biblical history: Rom. 13:9,13-14: "The commandments, 'You shall not commit adultery,' 'You shall not murder,' 'You shall not steal,' 'You shall not covet,' and whatever other command there may be, are summed up in this one command: 'Love your neighbor as yourself.' Let us behave decently, as in the daytime, not in carousing and drunkenness, not in sexual immorality and debauchery, not in dissension and jealousy. Rather, clothe yourselves with the Lord Jesus Christ, and do not think about how to gratify the desires of the flesh."

Think about the history of Israel. Over the centuries, when they obeyed God, He blessed and won battles for them. But every time they disobeyed, they were punished. Wouldn't you think they'd get the point and obey consistently?

But what about America today? God has undoubtedly had his hand on this nation over the centuries. But we daily see evidence that we want our way more and more and not God's way. We want God out of the picture except for an occasional magic wand sweep! And look where we are.

Wouldn't it be better to plan to obey and receive God's blessing? That's for the nation. But what about you?

"In the last days, perilous times will come..." I do not know if these are the last days, but it does seem they are progressing towards distressing problems.

Considering these thoughts on legalism, do you think it reasonable to practice planned obedience for both your own sake and for the sake of the gospel?

H. MODERN PHARISEES

This is a recap of a message shared by physician Dr. David Nesselrode and used with his permission. I often speak of the Pharisees and how there are many like them in today's Christian culture. Dr. Nesselrode grew up in the same atmosphere as me and did such an excellent job organizing his thoughts that I must share them with you. I take no credit for any of this. Only the last three brief paragraphs are my comments. In my first 60 years as a Christian, I was trapped in this mindset of the Pharisees and am now trying very hard to abandon it, and it is a slow process.

In the account of the Pharisee and the tax collector who came to Jesus to pray (Luke 18:9-14), each came with his agenda—the Pharisee trying to impress Jesus with his spirituality, and the tax collector admitting his lack of spiritual sensitivity. Only the tax collector left justified.

And how might we identify ourselves as Pharisees today? Try each of these on for size. I know I find myself guilty of far too many.

We might be a Pharisee if –

1. We love to point the finger and judge
2. We enjoy spreading news about the failures of others
3. We are good at sending people on a guilt trip
4. We require people to live up to standards not written in Scripture (Matt. 23:4)
5. We practice guilt by association
6. We assume something or someone is of the devil when their ministry makes us uncomfortable
7. We say a person is not a Christian if they disagree with us
8. We esteem "the way we've always done it" above change, even when the latter is not heresy (Jon Bush, the last seven words of a dying church are "We never did it that way before.")
9. We do not practice what we preach (Matt. 23:3)
10. We are more comfortable talking about the mighty movements of God of yesterday than today (Matt. 23:29-36)
11. We take ourselves too seriously
12. We judge by outward appearance (John 7:24)
13. We care more about people's opinions than God's
14. We need to be sure that people know about it if we give, pray, or fast (Matt. 6:1-4)
15. We are motivated by money (Luke 16:14)
16. We feel righteous by comparing ourselves to others rather than to the Word of God
17. We have no sense of sin by our thoughts, only our deeds (Matt. 15:11-12)
18. We major on minors (Matt. 23:23-24)
19. We are experts in finding what might seem to be loopholes in the Bible to excuse certain areas of disobedience (Matt. 15:3)
20. We are more concerned to uphold our theology than to help people
21. We love to score theological points with our enemies
22. We claim God's approval of us rather than our rivals because we "know" our theology, not theirs, is sound
23. We easily dismiss a person we don't like or disagree with because we are able to find something wrong with them
24. We say, "We are more in tune with God than you are"
25. We call another person a "Pharisee"

Clearly, scripture contains rules, regulations, standards, laws, and commandments. These are binding on those to whom they were specifically addressed and certainly shed light on issues that have changed either culturally or in the difference between OT and NT interpretation.

Our problem as legalists is that we attempt to clarify those issues by specifying more limitations that are/were not intended in the original restraints.

How did you score on that quiz? Hopefully, this devotional provokes some reflection and self-evaluation, like it has for me. If we truly let the Holy Spirit shine a light on the dark corners of our souls, we may discover that we're far more like the Pharisees than we like to think! I encourage you to let the Holy Spirit gently guide you to a place that firmly positions you closer to the tax collector and closer to the heart of God. We're on that journey together.

"It is for freedom that Christ has set us free. Stand firm, then, and do not let yourselves be burdened again by a yoke of slavery." (Gal. 5:1) Yes, we have been set free from the penalty of sin. But every translation I checked clarifies that we are not to be encumbered by rules and laws.

The entire 6th chapter of Romans makes it clear that we are not free to sin, rather, we are free from the power that makes us sin. We need to appropriate it.

Even Paul struggled with the old nature. (Romans 7:14-25) which concludes, "What a wretched man I am! Who will rescue me from this body that is subject to death?"

I once heard a marvelous message centered on the thought, "Man at his best is nothing." How many men or women have fallen in the area they considered under control in their lives?

Don't flaunt your freedom. Others may not be as strong spiritually and will be led astray. You'll be held responsible. (Romans 14:1-8) (I Cor. 8:13)

I do not profoundly regret what legalism did to me, but I deeply regret what it did to an untold number of people I have met through the years.

Perhaps in this culture, the opposite is license, so much so that there is little to distinguish a Christian from a non-Christian.

A reminder: I am writing this book with the sincere hope that you will not just read it like a newspaper or a novel. I hope that you will think. If you come up with a different conclusion than mine and have thought it through, I will have succeeded.

II Timothy 2:15 says, "Do your best to present yourself to God as one approved, a worker who does not need to be ashamed and who correctly handles the word of truth.." Are you conversant enough with scripture that you are not ashamed when someone questions you? Spend time studying. Do not be satisfied with just reading. (But read, too!)

CHAPTER

3

THE CHRISTIAN LIFE

When we give our lives to Christ, we are new creatures: the old life is gone, and the new life has begun. (II Cor 5:17) For some, the change is far less dramatic than for others who lived lives of debauchery. But we all have a new goal: to please the Lord.

Consider these verses:

- Eph. 4:1: "As a prisoner for the Lord, then, I urge you to live a life worthy of the calling you have received. Be completely humble and gentle; be patient, bearing with one another in love."
- James 1:22: "Do not merely listen to the word, and so deceive yourselves. Do what it says..."
- Phil. 4:8: "Finally, brothers and sisters, whatever is true, whatever is noble, whatever is right, whatever is pure, whatever is lovely, whatever is admirable—if anything is excellent or praiseworthy—think about such things."
- Galatians 5:16: "So I say, walk by the Spirit, and you will not gratify the desires of the flesh."
- I John 2:15-17: "Do not love the world or anything in the world. If anyone loves the world, love for the Father is not in them. For everything in the world—the lust of the flesh, the lust of the eyes, and the pride of life—comes not from the Father but from the world. The world and its desires pass away, but whoever does the will of God lives forever."

Currently, in America, we are looking at a cultural transformation, and what we find is that the culture is changing the church rather than the church changing the culture. Is Jesus the same yesterday, today, and forever, and is His word inerrant or not? 1 Corinthians 1:20-21: "Where is the wise person? Where is the teacher of the law? Where is the philosopher of this age? Has not God made foolish the wisdom of the world? For since in the wisdom of God the world through its wisdom did not know him, God was pleased through the foolishness of what was preached to save those who believe."

The more brilliant we think we are, the less we depend on the wisdom of God. Just think of the vast number of colleges and universities founded on thoroughly Biblical principles that now disavow the Bible. Or think of the denominations that started teaching the gospel and now hardly even refer to the Bible in their teachings except to prove their points.

I do not want to be guilty of taking a passage of scripture to make it say what I want it to say. I will agree that the primary message of the following verse is about very corrupt people, and I am not calling those who espouse Progressive Christianity corrupt—misled, not corrupt. Hear the words of Peter: "It would have been better for them not to have known the way of righteousness, than to have known it and then to turn their backs on the sacred command that was passed on to them." (II Peter 2:21) In I Peter 1:20, it says that no prophecy is for private interpretation. Most translations use the same word: prophecy. But does prophecy only mean foretelling the future, or can it mean teaching/preaching, as in the New Life translation (Holy Writings) or the Worldwide English translation (Holy Writings)?

Would you agree that we in America are headed in many wrong directions? Now, even our evangelical brothers and sisters are split.

I want to flesh out some of the issues related to your Christian life. What are they? How do we handle them?

A. CHOICES

"Choose my instruction instead of silver, knowledge rather than choice gold, for wisdom is more precious than rubies, and nothing you desire can compare with her." (Prov. 8: 10,11)

Decades ago, I heard a man preach on the following subject, and I have never forgotten it. The older I get, the more I see its truth: "Life is not determined by your desires but by the choices you make." Practice using wisdom rather than raw emotion or a knee-jerk reaction. Let that sink in. Think about it. Ponder it.

You can't have everything you want, so you must make some choices. You live with the results of those choices. Is it always necessary to go through the "School of Hard Knocks" to teach us what should have been obvious?

- Lifestyle: Will you run with the crowd characterized by activities that are spiritually and sociably on the risky side, or will you use good common sense and be more conservative? The results can be dramatically different.
- Marriage: I don't care to count the people I know who selected the wrong partner for life. Red lights were blinking during courtship, but emotions trumped good judgment. They're living with the results. But who dared to point out to that person what others were seeing but that individual was missing? Would that person have listened or told you to mind your own business?
- Vocation: How many people do you know who are employed below their potential or are just putting in the time to make a living because they didn't complete an education, or they failed to follow their dream, or they changed jobs so many times they missed all the benefits, or they can't find the perfect job, etc.? This has them stuck in a daily humdrum rather than enjoying their livelihood.
- Possessions: How many things do you need before you are satisfied? Just a few more? Meanwhile, other things in your life suffer...perhaps because you have to work multiple jobs to support your lifestyle...or you are so deep in credit card debt that interest payments consume your disposable income. Your greed or lack of patience has caused you to lose much of what you could have because you are paying interest instead of buying real value. You are paying the consequences of your choices.
- Eternal future: You're thinking, I'm a good person. God is love. I'm better than (fill in the blank)! However, the result is not based on your opinion of yourself or comparison to someone else's. There is a different standard. The Bible clearly says there is only one way to eternal life: through Jesus. (John 14:6) Any other option leads to everlasting death.

"You always do what you want to do. This is true with every act. You may say that you had to do something or were forced to, but whatever you do, you do it by choice. Only you have the power to choose for yourself." - W. Clement Stone

B. IF YOU WANT TO STAY HOT, GET CLOSE TO THE FLAMES

"Let us hold unswervingly to the hope we profess, for he who promised is faithful. And let us consider how we may spur one another on toward love and good deeds, not giving up meeting together, as some are in the habit of doing, but encouraging one another—and all the more as you see the Day approaching." (Hebrews 10:23-25)

Though many believers today do not recognize the importance of fellowship or local church involvement, Christian fellowship is essential to spiritual growth. Many aspects of our spiritual lives depend on being together with other believers to encourage, grieve, celebrate, teach, serve, and share life together.

People need community and need to be a part of something. When you withdraw from something, you lose interest. If you withdraw long enough, you will abandon a desire for that activity. On the other hand, when you are a part of a community, you are encouraged, motivated, and excited to participate. This is precisely why we are told to meet regularly with other Christians.

I want to support this view from a book by socialists Peter Burger and Thomas Luckman as quoted by Tony Campolo: "…the only way for an individual to maintain beliefs contrary to the dominant culture is to be a part of a close-knit, counter-cultural support group they call a 'plausibility structure,' wherein members meet regularly to reinforce and revitalize one another's beliefs and deconstruct all influences to the contrary. Within the group, they point out even convictions that might seem absurd to members of the dominant society, remain completely plausible, and in many cases virtually self-evident." Thus, even sociology proves that the Bible is correct and that we need to "meet together."

There are many ways to have a community as Christians. The most obvious is the church. There are also small groups in homes, Bible study groups at church or other venues, coffee houses, various types of rallies (particularly youth), and even choosing our closest friends wisely. Involvement in these activities does not save (convert) you, but it does seem to save (keep) you. To say you "believe' and are never with "believers" seems somewhat incongruent.

We must be careful that these occasions are not just social gatherings; rather, they always take place in the context of Christian values and thoughts in one form or another.

I have been involved in the Bible Conference/camping ministry for most of my adult life. This idea of community is a model for coming together with others of like faith and conviction to be revitalized and recharged. It is time purposed to draw us closer to our Lord while set apart in a relaxed vacation atmosphere.

Another reason we should be assembling in some planned structure is the issue of responding appropriately to scripture commands to care for the poor and disenfranchised. This does not have to be done through a formal church structure (including Sunday School class or Youth Group), but I am unaware it is done through house churches, home bible studies, etc. The church not only acquaints us with those opportunities at home and abroad but also has the best method of distributing money, food, clothing, etc. Secular organizations have so many "in-house" costs and high executive salaries that much of your dollar never reaches those for whom it was intended. I would include additional opportunities such as the local rescue mission, pregnancy center, food bank, etc.

The organized church also exposes people to a variety of mission opportunities around the world. First-person reports and periodic updates are provided on the achievement of previous giving to various individuals, organizations, or projects.

Going to church will never save your soul, but it may well save you from slipping and falling away from your faith or from abandoning your responsibility to society's poor and neglected and your mission of reaching the world.

I know nothing about birds, but I am told that geese can fly a 70% greater distance when they fly in formation rather than on their own. And do you know why they "honk"? To encourage one another! Is there a lesson there for us?

"To ensure that the self doesn't shrink, to see that it holds on to its volume, memories have to be watered like potted flowers, and the watering calls for regular contact with the witnesses of the past, that is to say, with friends." -Milan Kundera, Identity

"It is true, of course, that what is an unspeakable gift of God for the lonely individual is easily disregarded and trodden under foot by those who have the gift every day. It is easily forgotten that the fellowship of Christian brethren is a gift of grace, a gift of the Kingdom of God that any day may be taken from us... Therefore, let him who until now has had the privilege of living a common Christian life with other Christians praise God's grace from the bottom of his heart. Let him thank God on his knees and declare: It is grace, nothing but grace, that we are allowed to live in community with Christian brethren." — Boenhoffer, Life Together

C. FRIENDS

"Walk with the wise and become wise, for a companion of fools suffers harm." (Prov. 13:20)

Choose your friends wisely. They tell me a great deal about you.

After hiring a large summer staff for many years, early on, I discovered something: it takes about 3-5 days for friendships to form, and, by and large, the good ones get together, and the "bad apples" seem to find each other. "Friends are the family we choose for ourselves."- Edna Buchanan. Water seeks its own level.

I have no way of knowing whether you really trusted Christ; only He knows that. But I can get a rather good idea of your commitment to Him by watching your lifestyle.

If you claim Christ as your Savior but are more often surrounded by ungodly people than godly, you may need to begin to question your commitment to Christ. Would you rather be with God's crowd or the world's crowd? Walk with a skunk, smell like a skunk.

There is no suggestion here that you should have no unsaved friends. On the contrary, you are to be salt and light to them. How can you win them for Christ or be a good testimony for Him if you are not friendly with them?

The point is, where is your heart? On the one hand, Prov. 27:17 says, "As iron sharpens iron, so a friend sharpens a friend." On the other hand, James 4:4 says, "…It would have been better for them not to have known the way of righteousness, than to have known it and then to turn their backs on the sacred command that was passed on to them."

What kind of influence do your friends have on you? Do they draw you to the moral high ground or base feelings? Perhaps a better question is, what influence do you have on your friends? Are you at least open to discussion about your Christianity, or do you hope it never comes up in conversation?

If you are a good friend, somehow you will find an opportunity to share the good news and socialize with others who love the good news.

"Associate with men of good quality, if you esteem your own reputation; for it is better to be alone than in bad company." –George Washington

D. CONFRONTING HYPOCRISY

I am reassessing my past with the sincere desire to be more like Christ and less like a legalist. It seems that the more rules and regulations you lay out for "spirituality," the more you open the doors of your life for hypocrisy. It also gives you a specific checklist of things you must *not do* to be spiritual. For some reason, I have never seen a checklist of things we must do except have daily devotions (preferably first thing in the morning) and regularly go to church and Bible study or small group. Meet those criteria, and many other Biblical things don't *seem* to matter.

Unless I am totally biased and reading only things that already fit my "approved list," I think I can accurately say that the consensus of Christian literature concludes that the legalists of today are most closely illustrative of the Pharisees of Jesus' day. And He was very tough on them! Yet, I assume they seriously thought they were more spiritual than others.

"Then Jesus said to the crowds and to his disciples, 'the scribes and the Pharisees sit on Moses' seat, so do and observe whatever they tell you, but not the works they do. For they preach, but do not practice...'" Matt. 23:1-3.

The religious teachers had the rightful role as teachers and guardians of the Law. But they had no license to revise it or add to it. Their problem was that "They tie up heavy, cumbersome loads and put them on other people's shoulders, but they themselves are not willing to lift a finger to move them." (Matt. 23:4). They had developed a system of 613 laws, 365 negative commands, and 248 positive laws.

They were proud of their spirituality, and then Jesus struck the final blow with, "They do all of their deeds to be seen by others" (Matt. 23:5). They added so many clarifications of the Law that the Law was almost buried. Then, they paraded around as the spiritual elite.

Paul addresses the present Pharisees (legalists) in I Cor.4: 3-7. Space does not permit me to quote the passage, but I emphasize these words, "...learn not to exceed what is written, so that no one of you will become arrogant in behalf of one against the other."

Each of us is personally responsible for our actions. If we look to men (women) and pattern our spiritual lives after them, we have set ourselves up for great disappointment because we have so many different expectations that no one can live up to all of them.

The value of these verses is not to point out deficiencies in others, thus exalting ourselves, but to be used as a mirror to see ourselves for what we are.

Hypocrisy could easily be described as pretending to be something you are not. Does your behavior match your words? Do you live what you preach?

"Where one man reads the Bible, a hundred read you and me." D.L. Moody

E. WE JUST CAN'T GET IT RIGHT

"God saw all that he had made, and it was very good." (Gen. 1:31)

God made perfect man with free will, and man had only one rule to obey but didn't.

Man, at his best, doesn't get it right! We are flawed to the core.

- God initiated worship, and man began to worship stones, carvings, animals, the skies, etc.
- God created male and female, and the blessing of intimacy and man degraded it into depravity.
- God created government. Man abuses it for personal gain.
- God created a beautiful earth. Man abuses it for personal pleasure.
- God initiated marriage and family, and man distorted it.
- Man created weapons to survive and protect himself. Man turned them into instruments of destruction.
- Man created drugs for health/medicinal purposes. Man uses them for vile activities.
- Man created art. Man uses it for pornography and to induce base thinking.

"The heart is deceitful above all things, and desperately wicked: who can know?" (Jer. 17:9)

Even the great Apostle Paul said, "For we know that the law is spiritual: but I am carnal, sold under sin…For the good that I would I do not: but the evil which I would not, that I do…O wretched man that I am…!" (Rom: 7:14, 19, 24a) (KJV)

We all have the nature with which we were born. We take various psychological tests to determine if we are wired as Dominant, Influence, Steadiness, or Compliance (DISC).

Within each of those personalities, there are strengths and *weaknesses*. When we operate on all cylinders in any of those, Satan knows exactly where to attack. When under pressure, we naturally tend to fall back on the most significant *weakness* in that trait. And that is precisely where he attacks. So, we lose again, even at our best.

As the choir director, I was practicing with the choir just before the year's biggest concert. I overstepped the rehearsal deadline by about 90 seconds to allow a women's barbershop group that was to practice at 6:30pm. The director of that group came and *attacked* me. 90 seconds! I did not respond very kindly. I reacted; I didn't think. Bad! The worst came out. Some guests heard the exchange. Here's the clincher: I was also the pastor of the church!!!!! The guests attend the church!

We used to sing, "I need Jesus, need Him in the sunshine hour, need Him when the storm clouds lower. Every day along life's way, yes, I need Jesus." We also used to sing, "Take time to be holy." In this age and culture, we don't have enough time or take enough time to think about being holy. There are too many pressing issues. When we sing old hymns and any new contemporary songs related to honorable living, do we mean what we sing, or are they just lovely thoughts and tunes? Perhaps we should pay more attention.

Sin has consequences. I wish I could remember that each time I mess up...before I mess up. I need all the help I can get. "O wretched man that I am!" I need Jesus. I need to learn to take time to be holy. How about you?

Try as I might to put myself in the right place at the right time under the right circumstances, or, put the other way, do my best to stay out of places and situations that will bring on temptation, there almost always is a circumstance where there is a temptation: temper, lust, half-truths, greed, unkindness, conceit, etc. Satan jumps on it.

Get thee behind me, Satan, and stop pushing.

"We are too Christian to really enjoy sinning, and too fond of sinning to enjoy Christianity. Most of us know perfectly well what we ought to do; our trouble is that we do not want to do it." —Peter Marshall

F. A CHANGE OF FOCUS

I admit that I have a natural bent towards questioning what seems to me to be the ultra-spiritual over-statement of many things in the Bible. We make God say what He did not really say. I believe what the Bible says, not your interpretation of what you want it to say, to meet your purpose of the moment. The other day, I was in the Christian bookstore and saw a book called "Two Hundred Promises from God." I picked it up to glance through it, and it was filled with statements that were not promises at all!

But today, I want to leave my comfort zone and encourage you. I want to tell you some things you absolutely can do, no question about it. You can be a witness for Christ. I don't care how bashful, shy, or spiritually immature you feel.

You do not have to quote scripture or teach theology!

I am not asking or suggesting that you "attack for Jesus." Allow the conversation to take you there.

Has God been good to you? Tell someone how and why in normal conversation and see where it leads. One or two sentences will do. Perhaps you're just over an illness or just had a need met in a special way. Follow through if appropriate.

Do you pray before eating in a restaurant? Bow your head and pray. Someone will notice. Our friends make it a habit to say to the waitperson, "We always pray before we eat. Is there anything we might pray about for you?" Some of the responses are amazing! No one has ever declined!

Do you ever wear a tee shirt, sports shirt, sweater, jacket, or cap with printing or a logo? (I'll bet you guys have something with your favorite sports team on it!) This opens up all sorts of possibilities, some of them flat-out blatant. How about one that simply says, "I love my church." Several years ago, my wife and I were on a cruise. On a large ship, there were very few Afro-Americans. One older black couple stuck out: every day, each of them wore a different tee shirt with scripture, godly sayings, etc. You didn't have to guess whether they were Jesus-followers or not!

I have a sweater and a shirt printed on them, "Back to the Bible." I have a sweatshirt that says, "Sandy Cove." People ask where it is and what it is. When I tell them it is a Bible conference, as many times as not, they ask, "What is a Bible Conference?" Bingo! The same happens when people ask me what I did for a living. I tell them I was a Bible Conference Director. I have often gotten into a "travel" conversation and talked about being in India nine times. They ask why? Bingo! And the list goes on. It isn't difficult.

Do you have a Bible PROMINENTLY displayed in an obvious line of sight in your living room? Or are you reading a Christian book that can be readily seen while sitting around talking?

Could you have a license plate holder with a spiritual message or a decal that goes beyond saying, "I love my dog!" I suggest you do not have, "Honk if you love Jesus," and then drive like the devil!

I can't get by the verse that says, "Be ready always to give a reason for the hope that is within you." (I Peter 3:15) Did you notice that? Be ready to give an answer, a reason; that assumes someone will ask the question! What are you doing to prompt that question?

Jesus did not necessarily call you to be a preacher or teacher. He did call you to be an ambassador (II Corinthians 5:20), one who speaks for the one who sent him. That's you!

Do you want a deep feeling of satisfaction? If you want to be a witness, this will bring you great joy.

You can do it. YOU CAN DO IT! Go do it.

G. THE MEANING OF THE COMMA!

Perhaps I am a crusader for holding preachers/teachers to what I perceive to be realism in teaching the truths of scripture. There are exceptions to every generality, so I do not believe we can teach the generality to be taken literally for all time and all people. I must stress for the sake of clarity that I am referring to those who make wild promises and have wild expectations for us.

It seems we are to believe (and thus act) as if, for Christians closely following the Lord, there will be no stress or strain or heartbreak or disaster.

Here are several examples:

- I received a devotional recently from a very capable Bible teacher who went into the Greek to prove that we are never supposed to worry or be concerned. Jesus has us covered. I wonder if that person has ever heard of martyrs. They insist there are more martyrs at this very moment than ever before in history.
- Jesus will meet all of your **needs**. Did He do so for the dying believers around the world because of starvation?
- How about people with severe health problems? People prayed for them, and they were anointed with oil for healing. They were assured that if they had enough faith, they would be healed. But they died. Who did not have enough faith, those who prayed or the person being healed? The truth is that we all die sooner or later. If prayer would keep everyone from death, no one would ever die!!!
- How about someone who lost a job for no reason and cannot find another one of equal pay to sustain their budget?

I always feel that I must defend myself as being a Bible-believing, dedicated Christian. However, I live in the real world and see or hear of people who consistently have significant problems. And I can read! I do not see anyone without any issues.

One Sunday, our pastor gave what I believe to be a brilliant, realistic lesson on Christians and their problems: family, finances, health, interpersonal relationships, work, etc. It was so good that I want to share it with you, giving it my own twist…but giving him credit for the basic thoughts.

The Bible makes it clear that Paul had problems. Think of it: ten of the disciples died for their faith. We are told clearly that "in this world you will have trouble. But take heart! I have overcome the world." (John 16:33) Or this: "Brother will betray brother to death, and a father his child; children will rebel against their parents and have them put to death. You will be hated by everyone because of me, but the one who stands firm to the end will be saved. When you are persecuted in one place, flee to another. Truly I tell you, you will not finish going through the towns of Israel before the Son of Man comes." "The student is not above the teacher, nor a servant above his master. It is enough for students to be like their teachers, and servants like their masters. If the head of the house has been called Beelzebul, how much more the members of his household!" (Matt. 10:21-25)

Finally, Paul says in Philippians 1:29: "For it has been granted to you on behalf of Christ not only to believe on him, but also to suffer for him" and "we must go through many hardships to enter the kingdom of God." (Acts 14:22)

Listen to Paul in II Corinthians 4:8-9: "We are hard-pressed on every side, but not crushed; perplexed, but not in despair; persecuted, but not abandoned; struck down, but not destroyed."

We need to learn to trust. Trust is allowing someone to do something without fearing the consequences. We need to trust God on His terms, in His ways, and for His timing. The end result may not be what we had prayed for, but we trust that His ways are best.

The real issue is, do we trust God in the midst of the trouble? Someone said, "Jesus will meet you on the other side of the storm." Wrong! Jesus will go with you through the storm.

Let's visit our verses again and make a visual change:

We are hard-pressed on every side	,	but not crushed;
Perplexed	,	but not in despair;
Persecuted	,	but not abandoned;
Struck down	,	but not destroyed.

Notice the commas. Don't put a _period_ where God put a comma! You always go on after a comma: it is a pause to help you prepare for what is coming next. Just as temptation is not sin, rather the yielding to it is, so worry and concern are not sin. Instead, the yielding to them is. It's what you do on the other side of the comma. You _will_ have problems. You _will_ have occasion to fear, be worried, and be concerned because you are human. Trust, prayer, thankfulness, etc., are the bridges to cross the comma.

On which side of the comma are you living?

H. WORK AT IT

"Worship the Lord with gladness..." (Ps. 100:2a)

"Never be lacking in zeal, but keep your spiritual fervor, serving the Lord." (Rom. 12:11)

Malcolm Gladwell, in his book *Outliers*, coined what he calls the "10,000-Hour Rule." He argues that above a necessary level of aptitude—in whatever field or endeavor—the single most significant contributing factor to a person's success is the amount of time he or she spends working on it. "True mastery," he says, "is only achieved after ten thousand hours of effort, even for those who already possess the innate, baseline skill for it."

Think about how many times a basketball player shoots baskets. Or how many times a batter takes batting practice. Don't we all want a surgeon who has performed his specialty many, many times before we become the next patient? Don't you want an experienced pilot with many hours of flying time to be the pilot of your flight no matter how short?

It's the same way with Christian service. Given an ability, you become much more proficient as you practice it and put it to use, whether teaching Sunday School, leading the youth group, singing or playing solos, leading a Bible study, doing home visitation, preaching, etc. Practice makes perfect. Well, you'll never be perfect, but you'll be much better.

I know a young man who went into the pastorate with little speaking experience. He worked hard in preparation and then went into the woods and preached the sermon several times, attempting to "feel" it, refine it, and be comfortable presenting it. Today, he is a master communicator. I know another young man who desperately wanted to arrange music. It seemed he tried to put everything he knew into each arrangement in his early arrangements, which was very cumbersome. Today, years later, he is one of the most requested arrangers of Christian music in Nashville, and his name is widely known.

Learn the lesson today to take what you have and refine it. The Word says, "Whatever your hand finds to do, do it with your might." Ecclesiastes 9:10 "Whatever you do, work heartily, as for the Lord and not for humans." (Colossians 3:23) Your abilities can be highly improved if you work hard at them.

Remember that whatever you do, whatever your aptitude, it can be used to serve Jesus… here at home or on foreign fields. Office workers, carpenters, mechanics, teachers, medical personnel, etc., are desperately needed. Are you willing to refine those abilities for God's use?

"Who you are tomorrow begins with what you do today." — Tim Fargo

I. YOU KNOW YOU SHOULDN'T DO THAT!

Be honest. Remember that time or those times when you did something that your conscience, your good sense, your spiritual convictions screamed against? But you did it anyway! Cheating? Lying? Stealing? Adultery? Abuse? Cover-up? Some may be "small" and relatively inconsequential to everyone but you because it's between you and God (if it doesn't involve another person).

We all mean well and probably start well. But then a circumstance occurs that shakes our trust and belief that God is in control because He seems to be silent at the moment.

Consider Saul.

Tall, dark, handsome, strong, and a natural leader. Easily chosen by the people when they insisted on having a king like other nations had.

He started well, defeating the Philistines, Ammonites, Moabites, Amalekites, and Syrians. He wisely chose David as his second in command, but David's success led to Saul's eventual downfall. He was proud and enjoyed the accolades as king but became very jealous over David's success and popularity.

Drunk with power, he sought an answer from God regarding a pending invasion by the Philistines and went directly against God's command that forbade seeing a medium (soothsayer or witch). Saul had put all the witches and mediums out of the land once Samuel died. With Samuel, his mentor, gone and his life and kingdom breaking up, he disguises himself and visits the witch of Endor by night.

Remarkably, she recognizes him, and he swears by God, strictly contrary to the teaching of Lev. 20:27, that he will not harm her. She brings back Samuel's ghost, who tells Saul that the Philistines would conquer all of Israel. The next day in battle, Saul was severely wounded, and his sons were killed. Rather than be captured and tortured, Saul falls on his sword and dies.

Saul purposely ignored what he knew to be correct, probably because of his arrogance and influence. A boy with a slingshot and a pebble got his kingdom!

Circumstances of life sometimes overwhelm us, and we do what we know we should not do.

These are not all evil things at the core. Perhaps it was a desire to have a house, a car, a boat, or an expensive vacation that was way beyond what was reasonable for your income. Now you are suffering the consequences. Now you no longer can "afford" to tithe!

Perhaps you sinned in the past and have lied to cover-up.

Could it be that you cheated (or stole) and know that somehow you need to make it right?

Perhaps you cheated on your spouse. Is it better to go directly and confess, or wait until it becomes general knowledge and shames you even further plus bring grief to your entire family?

If only we believed "you may be sure that your sin will find you out." (Num.32:23) How much more proof do we need for that after looking at the present political, sports or religious world? And if you are a professed, born-again Christian, the standard is higher for you than anyone else!

Come clean now. The longer you wait the harder it will be.

"It is better to suffer once than to be in perpetual apprehension." Julius Caesar

J. GROWING IN THE LORD

I don't know how you acted growing up. I acknowledge, with regret, I always "pushed the envelope" on how far I could go and still be a "good boy." I had some nasty scrapes and near misses. Then I settled down, especially after getting married and joining full-time ministry. And do you know what I found (looking back)? The closer I tried walking with God (interpreted as the "more godly" I thought I became), the more judgmental I became. My expectations of others became more legalistic than my actual convictions. That's why I frequently call myself a recovering fundamentalist.

I thought the best way to please God was to live by the rules, some of which are set up in scripture, but most set up by man.

I want to thank Andy Stanley for these insights, clarifying what I have struggled with for so long. It is how I was taught by almost all of the preachers and teachers I know. Here it is, in essence—the Old Testament and the New Testament form the Bible, and it is all to be applied and obeyed. I found this created all sorts of problems for my questioning (rational?) mind. (I wrote a devotional more than a year ago about it, "Truthful Interpretation," centering around Psalm 91.)

But hear this and let me prove it.

Can you believe how we have overlooked what is so clear: we hear it repeatedly at communion, "This cup is the new covenant in my blood…". Remember, covenant and testament are the same: new covenant, New Testament. The New Testament (covenant) does not extend the old covenant (testament). It is new; it replaces, not extends, the old. Jesus said He came to "fulfill the law," bringing it to its designed end. When He said on the cross, "It is finished," what was finished? The old covenant. That game is over, and Jesus showed up at just the right time and won it. On with the new game. That doesn't mean that the Old Testament (old covenant) is not inspired or relevant, it means it is no longer applicable. Jesus gave us a new, better one. Think of it like this…the Old Testament is the question, and the New Testament is the answer. You will not fully appreciate the New Testament if you do not understand the Old Testament base on which it was built.

The Old Testament (old covenant) is great for history, inspiration, and illustration. It is directed to Israel. But don't go to it to apply. The New Testament, or the new covenant, the new way God deals with us, is not "obey and be blessed or disobey and be cursed" (in other words—a conditional covenant), but "receive grace and follow Christ's example of love" (an unconditional covenant). That doesn't mean there are no rules, but the new rules are based on Jesus' example of how to live as clarified in the new covenant, not the rules set up for the nation of Israel (old covenant).

You could be disappointed, frustrated or even angry by now, but read carefully:

Hebrews. 8:8, "But God found fault with the people (Israel) and said: 'The days are coming, declares the Lord, when I will make a new covenant with the people of Israel and with the people of Judah." But in fact the ministry Jesus has received is as superior to theirs as the covenant of which he is mediator is superior to the old one, since the new covenant is established on better promises. For if there had been nothing wrong with that first covenant, no place would have been sought for another. (It was predicted way back then!)

Hebrews 8:13, "By calling this covenant 'new,' he has made the first one obsolete; and what is obsolete and outdated will soon disappear. (Vanish away! Are you kidding me? Apparently it was supposed to disappear, but we haven't allowed it to.)

Hebrews 9:15, "For this reason Christ is the mediator of a new covenant, that those who are called may receive the promised eternal inheritance—now that he has died as a ransom to set them free from the sins committed under the first covenant."

Hebrews 12:24, "…to Jesus, the mediator of a new covenant, and to the sprinkled blood that speaks a better word than the blood of Abel (sacrificial system)."

This may be so new, such radical thinking, that I want to substantiate Hebrews 8:13 from other translations. In the interest of the length of this article, I have checked them all, and they all say the same thing.

Where is all this going? What am I trying to convey? I'm thinking, learning, clarifying, substantiating what I believed all along but could not put into words even though the words were right in front of me…for years! They just didn't register because they didn't fit my preconceived notion.

Here's the conclusion from another highly respected Christian leader, Jim Cymbala: "No command or promise in the Old Testament can be applied to Christians today unless it is found repeated and illustrated in the New Testament." To be more specific, nine out of the ten commandments are reiterated and illustrated in the new covenant (observing the Sabbath is left out because the temple is now inside of us), and "the Law" is summed up in one verse: "'Love the Lord your God with all your heart and with all your soul and with all your mind.' This is the first and greatest commandment. And the second is like it: 'Love your neighbor as yourself.' All the Law and the Prophets hang on these two commandments." (Matt. 22: 37-40)

Think back to some of my opening words: "I settled down, especially after getting married and becoming a part of full-time ministry." Allow me to translate that. My love for my wife tamed my behavior. She didn't write me a set of rules. My love of the ministry dictated my behavior, but it was primarily pleasing people, thus pleasing God. Since retirement, when I no longer had to please people for the ministry's good, my love of Jesus dictates my behavior and no longer mirrors a set of "don'ts" expected by my clientele. I try to be careful not to offend others by my actions, not because they interpret differently, but because I love them enough to honor them. Love (unconditional love, a relationship) changes everything.

How about you? What do you think?

K. JUST ABIDE

Abide. Somehow, I don't ever remember hearing that word except in a spiritual context. So, if we don't use it much in normal conversation, what does it mean?

According to the dictionary, it means to dwell or remain. That means I abide in, dwell in, remain in Florida. That means my life is focused in Ft. Myers. I go other places for various reasons, but I always go back home, and there's no place like home.

Keep that in mind as you read Psalm 15 which tells us who may abide with the Lord.

"Lord, who may abide in, dwell in, be at home in your sacred tent? Who may live on your holy mountain? The one whose (1) *walk is blameless*, who (2) *does what is righteous*, who (3) *speaks the truth from his* <u>*heart*</u>; whose (4) *tongue utters no slander*, who (5) *does no wrong to a neighbor*, and (6) *who despises a vile person but honors those who fear the Lord*; who (7) *keeps an oath even when it hurts* and does not change his mind; who (8) *lends money to the poor without interest*; who (9) *does not accept a bribe against the innocent*." (Amplified Bible)

That's quite a list. And here's the conclusion, "Whoever does these things will never be shaken."

You may, of necessity, function in the marketplaces of life—work, school, entertainment, socializing—but remember where you abide, where it's good to be back home.

Do you want to have an impact for God, in many cases not even saying a word, but living a Godly lifestyle? "Remain in me, as I also remain in you. No branch can bear fruit by itself; it must remain in the vine. Neither can you bear fruit unless you remain in me." (John 15:4)

JUST ABIDE

Is your day's load heavy? Just abide.
And the day's road stony? Just abide.
If your heart is growing weary,
And your sky is gray and dreary,
Just abide and keep on abiding.
—John R. Clements

Psalm 91:1: "Whoever dwells in the shelter of the Most High will rest in the shadow of the Almighty."

L. HE WAS A GOOD MAN

Lot and Abraham moved to Canaan, and a famine forced him back to Bethel. Their flocks multiplied rapidly and their herdsmen began to quarrel. Abraham suggested they separate and gave Lot the choice of the land available. Lot chose the best of the two options, but it was a poor choice because he was taken captive by four kings in the area. Upon hearing this, Abraham took his trained men to rescue him. They recovered all their goods and brought Lot and all who had been captured.

Lot then married a woman of Sodom, the most wicked city mentioned in Scripture. God rescued him again just before Sodom was burned to the ground. But his wife looked back and died. So, he committed incest with his daughters, from whom descended the wicked nations of Ammon and Moab. (Genesis 11:31-14:16; 19:1.)

Now hear II Peter 2:5-9: "And he (God) did not spare any of the people who lived in ancient times before the flood except Noah, the one man who spoke up for God, and his family of seven. At that time God completely destroyed the whole world of ungodly men with the vast flood. Later, he turned the cities of Sodom and Gomorrah into heaps of ashes and blotted them off the face of the earth, making them an example for all the ungodly in the future to look back upon and fear. But at the same time *the Lord rescued Lot out of Sodom because he was a good man,* sick of the terrible wickedness he saw everywhere around him day after day. *So also the Lord can rescue you and me* from the temptations that surround us, and continue to punish the ungodly until the day of final judgment comes."

Despite his initial resistance and moral failure, the Scripture describes Lot as a "good man," a "righteous man." Lot belonged to the Lord, and God's grace and mercy continued to be his experience. God saw that he was "sick of the terrible wickedness he saw everywhere around him day after day." (9)

Lot a good man? Don't ask me to explain it but let me tell you in no uncertain terms that I am grateful for whatever is in the heart and mind of God to look with favor on me even after I have sinned repeatedly and perhaps even grievously. God knows my spirit, which seems like a matter of the heart. He knows my weakness. He knows how to deliver and rescue me from the evil surrounding me. He knows how I desire to please Him.

As perplexing as Lot's situation might be, we also see God's grace in our lives.

M. YOUR LEGACY

Someone smarter than I said, "It's not what you gather, but what you scatter that tells what kind of life you have lived."

If that means that what you consciously did to help, encourage, and stimulate people, I'm in bad shape. Looking back, I was so busy making things happen, that I didn't even consider the concept. My adult life was lived with deadlines: weekly choir numbers for church and radio, concert deadlines, solving financial crises, radio deadlines, daily staff challenges, family responsibilities, etc. My type A personality, a driver, was always focused on the next thing. It took me at least 10 years of retirement to slow down!

But, despite that, I did some things, albeit unintentionally in many cases, for which I am so grateful.

I have a wonderfully loving and supportive wife and three children who follow the Lord. I know many who were in similar ministry situations who cannot say that. I am thankful.

Many people with whom I was associated in a leadership role are now in various areas of ministry: music, camping, pastors and teachers, etc. Now and then I receive another note from someone thanking me for my influence on their lives, and I never really knew it. Many of them have exceeded my accomplishments by far, which excites me.

Two days ago, I received a book written by Phil Burks— "How to Eat a Failure Sandwich." Phil was in our youth group at church, worked for me at Sandy Cove. He is now a multi-millionaire businessman in TX. In the book, he mentions how I influenced him. I had no idea! I knew we were good friends, but I never knew what he felt.

I thank God that I scattered at least a little.

Recently, I wrote a devotional concerning encouragement and how I need all the help I can get. I am attempting to contact people I know who need encouragement just to tell them I'm praying for them by name virtually every night. Within 15 minutes of sending the email, I heard from an old friend, Walt Wiley, who founded a ministry he calls, "Winning With Encouragement." He sent me a book which he just completed entitled, "Encouragement: The Art of Giving…The Joy of Receiving." It is a very easy read and worthwhile every second you spend in it. (I include nothing from it in this devotional.) Walt frequently speaks at Sandy Cove.

We lived very interesting lives in terms of gatherings. Now, in our retirement years, we are probably the least financially endowed of any of our friends. But we've traveled the world in ministry (and for pleasure), and as we look in our closets, there is nothing we need. We never have to worry about getting enough money for food or shelter. God has met every need (and beyond). Shell Point and the security we have here are excellent.

I am not looking for troublesome days in the future, but in advanced age, it is improbable that this will not occur. I remember so well a Sandy Cove speaker and friend, a pastor, who was diagnosed with an incurable disease. One Sunday, following the news, he stood before his congregation and said, "I have been showing you how to live; now I want to show you how to die." That would also be my prayer when, and if, that time comes. I repeat, I'm not looking forward to such a time. I would love to die in my sleep!

So, what is the point of this devotional? I assure you it is not to glorify myself. It is to assure you that people are watching you. They are. That's a fact. Maybe someday you will get notes or mentions in a book and are surprised as I was.

What is your legacy?

N. GODLINESS

I've been thinking about godliness and want to do an honest self-assessment. Perhaps another word might be spirituality. Whatever the word, how do I meet the criteria? In fact, what are the requirements?

My heart desires to be in a position of continual growth toward spiritual maturity in my Father's eyes. How do I determine that? This is a lengthy subject that may be a bit difficult to unravel. Someone asked, "How do you eat an elephant?" The answer is, "One bite at a time."

Will you share my journey for your own self-evaluation? I want to share my thoughts with you, and I don't want you to read through it without much thought.

This is the product of hours of thinking and processing. There is no attempt at a logical sequence—just thoughts concerning several areas of lifestyle. So, let's begin.

O. THE PROBLEM OF ANGER

Even the nicest people sometimes go over the edge and get angry. Many people are good at covering it up on the outside but are boiling on the inside. Most of us, when experiencing the "blow-up," did it spontaneously, and moments later, we are humiliated on the inside, desperately wishing we could take it all back to respond more appropriately.

The problem with many preachers or would-be preachers who are trying to guilt trip us is that they fail to consider what the Scriptures say in their entirety. So, let's look at some passages on anger. I acknowledge much assistance in this study to the writings of Dr. Jay Adams, psychologist, and Rev. David Pratte.

The Bible specifically says, "Be angry and do not sin" (Ephesians 4:26). Apparently, some anger is justifiable.

1. God is angry with sin. (Psalm 7:11; John 3:36; Romans 1:18; 2:5-9; Ephesians 5:6; Colossians 3:6) If God is angry with sin, we can be (should be?) too!
2. There are many examples of Moses being and acting angry because of sin. (Exodus 11:4-8; 32: 19-24; Numbers 12:3; 16:15)

3. Jesus was angry with sin. (Mark 3:5)
4. Paul and a whole congregation of people acted with "indignation" towards one of their members who had sinned. (I Corinthians 5)

But we still have a problem: most of us suffer from anger that has little to do with sin but rather with what affects us personally, our feelings and egos. And there's the danger.

In Matthew 5:22 from the Sermon on the Mount Jesus taught, "He who is angry at his brother without a cause is in danger of judgment." Note: without cause. Apparently, there are causes which are not sin!

James 1:19 & 20 says, "My dear brothers and sisters, take note of this: Everyone should be quick to listen, slow to speak and slow to become angry because human anger does not produce the righteousness that God desires.." Note: be slow! Proverbs 14:17 says, "A quick-tempered man does foolish things..." (See also Proverbs 29:22.) Again, it would seem there is a time when anger is justified. The issue is to determine when it is appropriate and when it is not.

"Getting it out of your system" or "releasing the tension" by venting is a terrible idea.

So is "clamming up" because that eventually leads to the "blow up." Sinful thoughts lead to sinful actions. While Ephesians 4 tells us that all anger is not sin, it does say that we should put away the anger associated with "bitterness, loud quarreling, evil speaking, and malice."

Remember that your anger can be controlled. God commands it, and He does not expect us to do the impossible, so there must be a way! I Corinthians 10:13 assures us that we do not face any temptation that is beyond our ability to handle, for God will make a way of escape.

Many passages in the Scriptures refer to self-control. Likewise, they tell us to control our tempers: I Corinthians 9: 25-27; II Peter 1: 5-8; Galatians 5: 22,23.

How can you learn to handle anger?

1. Study the Scripture passages mentioned in this document. Fix them in your mind. Think of them just when you are ready to "blow your top"!
2. Repent of each incident when you were angry and pray for self-control in the future.

3. Stay away from people or situations that tend to "set you off" as much as possible! When necessary, prepare yourself and overlook what would normally upset you. Practice self-control!
4. Force yourself to think about the consequences of your anger. Be slow to act!
5. Reject a mindset of revenge for those who have injured you. Forgive and forget. Use your energy to fix the problem rather than to perpetuate the problem.
6. Be willing to listen to the advice of other Godly people.

We all have been told that harboring anger is much more destructive to us than the person we are angry with. We spend our time fussing and fuming, scheming and conniving, and the other person goes on his merry way with no thoughts or concerns! In the final analysis, it does come down to the fact that we were the losers by holding on to the anger! Winston Churchill said, "By swallowing evil words unsaid, no one has ever harmed his stomach." How much better would it be to go to the person humbly to solve the problem? If the other person rejects your offer, you have done your part and can forget it from there. It is off your conscience.

Anger is not good. Neither is it always sin. May God give us the wisdom and determination to differentiate between them and to deal with them wisely.

P. PEOPLE ARE DIFFERENT

Each of us is unique. Some are detail-oriented, and some are broader brush-oriented. Some are more fact-oriented, others more emotional. Some are more self-focused, others more other-centered. There is no "right" style. Each style has good and bad aspects.

There must be a set of criteria applicable to all styles. Anyone who feels spiritually superior has already disqualified himself from being a fair adjudicator. Pride is a sin; spiritual pride is obnoxious to the human observer and must be disdainful to the Lord.

How honest and open can we be when we look only at ourselves and do not compare ourselves to others around us? It would be easy to judge ourselves against others, but they are not the standard. This self-examination must eliminate all others and be totally self-focused.

Q. STRUGGLE

I am intensely interested in astronomy and God's incredible handiwork in creation. Recently, I was reading an article that contained the following quote: "It doesn't seem to me that this fantastically marvelous universe, this tremendous range of time and space and different kinds of animals, and all the different planets, and all these atoms with all their motions, and so on, all this complicated thing can merely be a stage so that God can watch human beings struggle for good and evil…. The stage is too big for the drama." — Richard Feynman, physicist

If I may interpret that in my own words, such a great God would not create man and then allow him to struggle with good and evil. He is too big and caring for that.

This physicist needs to get his head out of the books and equations and focus on what is around him…struggle…on every side, above and beneath!

Countries struggle. For some, it's poverty, flood or draught, war, or internal turmoil.

Mothers struggle to give birth (animals, too), children struggle to learn to walk, students struggle to gain knowledge, athletes struggle to be physically and mentally capable of their tasks; the list is endless.

As we watched our infant children struggle to stand upright and later balance on roller and ice skates, then ride their bicycles, drive a car, swim, and learn the times tables, among countless other struggles, we helped them but didn't do it for them because we knew that if accomplished, they would gain confidence and build on it in the future, becoming mature, responsible adults.

Perhaps that's why wise, loving, caring parents insist that their children struggle through algebra, Latin, college, and even possible financial stress.

Some people struggle with obesity, and others are underweight. Some people struggle because of birth defects or inherited physical flaws. Many people struggle because of a lack of mental acuity or mental illness.

People struggle with addictions: alcohol, drugs, sexual.

How many great men and women, both spiritual and secular, have written that gaining victory over struggle is/was the best growing experience of their lives? In life, few satisfactions surpass the feeling of accomplishment produced by successfully overcoming struggles. You will find joy in overcoming obstacles. The greater the obstacle, the more glory in overcoming it.

Here are selected verses concerning what the Bible says about struggles:

"No temptation has overtaken you except what is common to mankind. And God is faithful; he will not let you be tempted beyond what you can bear. But when you are tempted, he will also provide a way out so that you can endure it." (1 Corinthians 10:13) "Consider it pure joy, my brothers and sisters, whenever you face trials of many kinds, because you know that the testing of your faith produces perseverance. Let perseverance finish its work so that you may be mature and complete, not lacking anything.." (James 1:2-4) ":..And endurance (through struggles) produces proven character, and proven character produces hope." (Romans 5:4) (HCSB)

In the Bible, our first parents, Adam and Eve, struggled with temptation. They lost, and we inherited their nature, just as you inherit certain characteristics physically and mentally from your parents.

If I were a betting man, I would wager that the above-mentioned intellectual struggles with the concept of God because He cannot be boiled down to a system, equation, or formula. So, assuming himself superior, he makes himself his own God. And if he were God, we'd all be in a heap of trouble.

But God, in His infinite love, gave the example of His Own Son, Who endured the greatest struggle of all torture and sacrifice of His own life to atone for the struggles that His children could never conquer on our own, the struggle to obtain eternal life.

God must have intended when He presented the universe to mankind, foreknowing all of its consequent miseries and pain, that the struggle to overcome each obstacle would inevitably produce an awareness of man's ultimate need to depend on Him in everything.

Struggle is not enjoyable, but when handled properly, it is beneficial.

R. UNINTENDED CONSEQUENCES

The law of unintended consequences is that our actions always have unanticipated or unintended effects. Economists and other social scientists have heeded its power for centuries; politicians and popular opinion have largely ignored it for just as long.

There is only one difference between a bad economist and a good one: the bad economist confines himself to the *visible* effect; the good economist takes into account both the effect that can be seen and those effects that must be *foreseen*.

The law of unintended consequences is at work always and everywhere. Our future is determined not by our dreams but by our choices.

The Bible has a law of unintended consequences also. It is simple to understand. "Be sure your sins will find you out." (Numbers 22:33) Yes, that is in the Old Testament and written to Israel, but there are 91 other verses in the Bible on the same subject!

I can't tell you how many times that has stopped me. When traveling (years ago), I had to push myself away (mentally) from the magazine stores. When in the hotel, I had to force myself past specific channels. Age changes your temptations. How honest are you with your finances? What do you watch on TV, the internet, and in-home movie rentals? What do you read? Are you really what other people think you are? What are you like when no one is watching?

Each of these could be applied to everyday life very easily. For example, what if my wife came in on me when I was watching pornography? Or what if I was caught in a bald-faced lie that all my family knew about? Is it worth the result? What are the unintended consequences? Personal shame, hurt to family, possible loss of job, a short moment of pleasure followed by months or years of regaining credibility.

But here's the marvelous news, "My dear children, I write this to you so that you will not sin. But if anybody does sin, we have an advocate with the Father—Jesus Christ, the Righteous One. He is the atoning sacrifice for our sins, and not only for ours but also for the sins of the whole world." (I John 2: 1,2) Please don't take that as a license to sin or take it lightly. Read it closely. It says he is writing so that they will not sin!

The Bible and God Himself acknowledge that we are not perfect but are to be maturing, which indicates that we are aware of some things that must be eliminated.

I had a friend, now deceased, who always preached, "Count to 10 before reacting and ask yourself—what difference will it make 10 years from now?" Perhaps that is a bit impractical, but it does cause a pause before acting.

Look out! The law of unintended consequence will catch up to you. Be sure your sin will find you out…sometimes after you are dead when you have no chance to repent and rebuild your reputation.

Sandy Cove

Sandy Cove Choralaires and Brass, circa 1983

Sandy Cove Summer Staff, circa 1983

Gull Lake Bible and Missionary Conference, Hickory Corners, MI

Gull Lake Conference Activity

Concert in Miller Auditorium, Kalamazoo, MI, circa 1987

Indian Creek Choir, Ft. Myers, FL, circa 2013

CHAPTER

4

WITNESSES

- Acts1:8
"But you shall receive power when the Holy Spirit has come upon you; and you shall be witnesses to Me in Jerusalem, and in all Judea and Samaria, and to the end of the earth."

- Matthew5:14-16
"You are the light of <u>the world</u>. A city that is set on a hill cannot be hidden. Nor do they light a lamp and put it under a basket, but on a lampstand, and it gives light to all *who are* in the house. Let your light so shine before men, that they may see your good works and glorify your Father in heaven."

- 1Peter2:9
"But you *are* a chosen generation, a royal priesthood, a holy nation, His own special people, that you may proclaim the praises of Him who called you out of darkness into His marvelous light;"

- Matthew10:32-33
"Therefore whoever confesses Me before men, him I will also confess before My Father who is in heaven. But whoever denies Me before men, him I will also deny before My Father who is in heaven."

- John15:26-27
  "But when the Helper comes, whom I shall send to you from the Father, the Spirit of truth who proceeds from the Father, He will testify of Me. And you also will bear witness, because you have been with Me from the beginning."

A witness for Jesus follows his teachings through acts of compassion, justice, worship, and devotion, guided by the Holy Spirit.

Let's be candid: witnessing for Christ is frightening. It makes us feel vulnerable because we fear we won't have logical answers to real questions. Most of us feel a terrible sense of inadequacy. Sometimes, we even feel we'll be mocked, belittled, or ridiculed. We do not want to be embarrassed or demeaned by others.

Therefore, I would conjecture that most of us don't do it *intentionally* very often. We have all sorts of opportunities, but we allow them to pass for the above reasons.

Our pastor mentioned in his sermon that he went to the local shopping mall and sat on a bench for more than an hour and a half specifically to "witness." He simply sat there until someone else sat down and then began a simple conversation. As appropriate, he asked a simple question, "How do you get God to like you more?" Some people got up and left; others offered the answers you might expect: go to church regularly, be good (moral), be more honest, etc. Once they answered, he told them they couldn't do anything; God already loved them and proved it by sending Jesus to die for their sins. Obviously, he used scripture to prove his point. You know and can quote John 3:16. What's wrong with that one as a starter? You might also know Romans 5:8, "But God demonstrates his own love for us in this: while we were still sinners, Christ died for us." That's certainly short enough to remember!

But, you're thinking, he's a preacher! I'm not. Precisely. And witnesses don't have to preach. Witnesses tell what they have seen, heard, or experienced. People may not like it, but they cannot deny your story. What was (is) your experience with Christ? That's YOUR story.

"You are my witnesses" (Acts 1:8), and it says to begin at home, then your area, then your state, and then the whole world. Tell your story. Someone just might be intrigued and pursue the conversation.

Paul said in II Corinthians 5: 11, 14, and 20 that we should "try to persuade others" because "Christ's love compels us" and "we are therefore Christ's ambassadors." Ambassadors represent their country in another country; we represent Christ in another ethos.

In fact, you don't need to say a word to witness! A pastor friend frequently uses this quote: "Witness to everyone you meet, in every situation, at all times. And, if necessary, use words."

Have you ever considered wearing a tee shirt with a Bible verse or scriptural saying? Or one that names your church or Christian organization? People may be curious and ask about it. I have a hat that has "Morning Cheer" on it. That's the legal name of the ministry with which I was associated. I was on an elevator one morning and a fellow who hadn't recovered from the night before looked at it and said, "I've never heard of that drink before"! Bingo! My elevator speech! It takes 5 seconds. "Morning Cheer is a ministry that operates a Bible Conference and camp where Christians meet for vacation and spend time in the Bible learning more about Jesus."

Do you send out Christmas cards or letters? Do they specifically talk about the Christ-child? Does your Christmas letter even mention Jesus? How can you call yourself a Christian and celebrate the birthday of Jesus without even talking about Him?

Do you invite your unsaved friends to a concert where you know Jesus will be proclaimed?

Do you invite your unsaved friends to your church at Christmas, Easter, or for a special program? Will they hear gospel message there? If not, you'd better find another church!

The Bible says that we as believers should be ready always to give an answer for our faith to those who ask. (I Peter 3:15) That presumes that you are giving people a reason to ask! Are you? What better, easier time than Christmas?

In Luke 2: 8-20, I offer these excerpts: "There were shepherds watching their locks...an angel came upon them and told them of the birth of Jesus...then a heavenly host appeared... the shepherds decided to check out the news they heard ...they left their flocks and found the baby...and after they saw him they returned, glorified God and **told everyone.**" (KJV)

Did you find Him? What are you going to do about it? Who are you going to tell? How?

Now you think about that!

A. A CHANGE OF FOCUS

I admit that I have a natural bent towards questioning what seems to me to be the ultra-spiritual over-statement of many things in the Bible. We make God say what He did not actually say. I believe what the Bible says, not your interpretation of what you want it to say to meet your purpose of the moment. The other day, I was in the Christian bookstore and saw a book called *Two Hundred Promises from God.* I picked it up to glance through it, and it was filled with statements that were not promises at all!

But today, I want to leave my comfort zone and encourage you. I want to change my focus. I want to tell you some things you absolutely can do; there is no question about it. You can be a witness for Christ. I don't care how bashful, shy, or spiritually immature you feel.

You do not have to quote scripture or teach theology!

I am not asking or suggesting that you "attack for Jesus." Allow the conversation to take you there.

Has God been good to you? In everyday conversation, tell someone how and why and see where it leads. One or two sentences will do. Perhaps you're just over an illness or just had a unique need met. Follow through if appropriate.

Do you pray before eating in a restaurant? Bow your head and pray. Someone will notice. We have friends who make it a habit to say to the waitperson, "We always pray before we eat. Is there anything we might pray about for you?" Some of the responses are amazing! No one has ever declined!

Do you ever wear a tee shirt, sports shirt, sweater, jacket, or cap with printing or a logo on it? (I'll bet you guys have something with your favorite sports team on it!) This opens up all sorts of possibilities, some of them flat-out blatant. How about one that says, "I love my church." Several years ago, Mary Esther and I were on a cruise. On a large ship, there were very few Afro-Americans. One older couple stuck out: every day, each wore a different tee shirt with scripture, godly sayings, etc. You didn't have to guess whether they were Jesus-followers or not!

I have a sweater and a shirt printed on them, "Back to the Bible." I have a sweatshirt that says, "Sandy Cove." People ask where it is and what it is. When I tell them it is a Bible conference, as many times as not, they ask, "What is a Bible Conference?" Bingo! The same happens when people ask me what I did for a living. I tell them I was a Bible Conference Director. I have often gotten into a "travel" conversation and talked about being in India nine times. They ask why. Bingo! And the list goes on. It isn't difficult.

Do you have a Bible PROMINENTLY displayed in an obvious line of sight in your living room? Or are you reading a Christian book that can be readily seen while sitting around talking?

Could you have a license plate holder with a spiritual message or a decal that goes beyond saying, "I love my dog!" I suggest you do not have, "Honk if you love Jesus," and then drive like the devil!

I can't get by the verse that says, "Be ready always to give a reason for the hope that is within you." (I Peter 3:15). Did you notice that? Be ready to give an answer. That assumes someone is going to ask the question! What are you doing to prompt that question?

Jesus did not necessarily call you to be a preacher or teacher. He did call you to be an ambassador (II Corinthians 5:20), one who speaks for the one who sent him. That's you!

Do you want a deep feeling of satisfaction? If you want to be a witness, this will bring you great joy.

You can do it. YOU CAN DO IT! Go do it.

B. WHO DO YOU REMEMBER?

My wife and I have thousands of pictures from our past, which we occasionally sort through and cull. And which pictures are culled? Those that are duplicates or no longer meaningful.

Suppose I considered only those persons on the musical staff at the two conferences where I was musical director and worked with them two hours a day at least six days a week. In that case, the total number of people might be 150-200. And who do I remember? Those who were good and those who were challenging for one reason or another. That means that even seeing the picture of some of them, I cannot give you a name, incident, or anecdote about them. They were there, participated, and primarily added bodies, not musical strength. (I recall two sopranos I could not even hear when they each had their own microphones!)

I might add that this also says something about me: I was more interested in results than people! Not good! I can make excuses for that by saying my responsibility was to deliver a quality program at the end of each week, not be a bosom buddy for life. Or that the musical group was only one part of my daily responsibility. But that's at least, in part, a coverup for being more results-oriented than people-oriented.

Imagine living in such mediocrity that there are no signs of your existence; people don't remember you and can't put a name to your face, even with a picture.

It is also interesting to note that many problematic people were very successful. They matured and focused rather than just drifting into patterns of mediocrity and blending into the scenery. On the other hand, some very gifted people did not end well. Those in the middle just disappeared from my radar. One fellow had a good voice but did everything horribly from a vocal standpoint, went on to college, and became nationally known in a Christian group. Another who was a real discipline challenge became a jungle missionary pilot for many years!

We live in a purpose-driven culture that has robbed us of the gift of meaning and substituted the urgency of purpose for it. We men usually ask, "And what did you do for a living?" within the first few sentences after meeting someone new, OR we include his accomplishments in the introduction to that person. Focusing on the person rather than the attainment would make us more intimate and fascinating. It is natural to want to speak or read about yourself! We all wish we could make a difference of some kind. We all want to be remembered.

All of that to say this: Matthew 7 tells the story of people who were involved with religious works around well-meaning projects. Verse 20 reminds us that we are known by the fruit we produce, and verse 27 tells us that only those who build their house upon the rock will survive the storm. To those who were just involved for their satisfaction, He said, "I never knew you." In essence, you were just there; you made no effectual contribution; end of subject.

Ron Cline preached five messages on "The Parade," in which he described all of the people and paraphernalia going down the street while thousands sat along the sidewalk just watching. Nameless spectators. They were a part of the event but not contributors. He likened it to our mission involvement and suggested many ways to become involved rather than just being spectators.

Is your contribution just your presence or something of meaning and substance for which you will be remembered and rewarded?

C. TELL YOUR LIFE STORY

"Only be careful, and watch yourselves closely so that you do not forget the things your eyes have seen or let them fade from your heart as long as you live. Teach them to your children and to their children after them."—Deuteronomy 4:9

Many people care greatly about ensuring that their resources are used well after death. They set up trusts, write wills, and establish foundations to guarantee that their assets will continue to be used for a good purpose after their life on earth is done. We call this good stewardship.

Equally important, however, is being good stewards of our life story. God commanded the Israelites not only to teach their children His laws but also to make sure they knew their family history. Parents and grandparents were responsible for ensuring their children knew the stories of how God had worked on on their behalf. (Deut. 4)

God has given each of us a unique story. His plan for our lives is individualized. Do others know what you believe and why? Do they know the story of how you came to faith and how God has worked in your life to strengthen your faith? Do they know how God has shown Himself faithful and has helped you through doubts and disappointments?

I encourage you to do this, especially for your extended family. Write or type it out. Perhaps you have never shared your faith journey with a family member. This is a painless, subtle way of accomplishing that. Who knows what reaction may begin in that person's mind and heart?

Here are some other areas that may be of interest and may capture their attention enough to read it to the end, but most importantly, tell them about your faith journey and relationship with the Lord.

1. What was the most exciting day of your life?
2. What was the worst day of your life?
3. What would you do differently if you could go back and start all over again?
4. How did you meet your mate?
5. How much were some of your earliest expenses (food, gasoline, car, house or rent), etc.
6. How much was your first annual income?
7. Why did you choose the specific institution for your education?
8. Why do you attend the church you chose?
9. Why did you choose to go to the retirement center that you now call home, or why are you staying in your present abode rather than moving/downsizing/ etc.?

Those are just a start. You'll have better ideas about your own life.

D. HOW CAN GOD USE YOU?

Perhaps you think you are nobody. You have nothing to offer. You are a broken vessel—someone with a physical handicap. You are too old. You are too [something].

Jonathan Edwards was extremely nearsighted and squinted over his sermon, holding the pages close to his face so he could see the words. He read each page and chosen phrase carefully with an unimposing monotone voice. But God's Spirit moved through Jonathan Edwards' preaching to fan the First Great Awakening revival fires and bring thousands to faith in Christ.

While certainly not to be compared to Jonathan Edwards, Ralph Keiper was blind in one eye and extremely nearsighted in the other. He was a researcher for the famous Donald Grey Barnhouse of the 10th Presbyterian Church in Philadelphia and a noted expositor. Keiper had to hold his notes very close to his face and used them only as a guide. He had deeply researched messages and a great sense of humor. Assembled crowds loved him and his teaching. His life and ministry touched untold thousands.

Cordell Brown was born with cerebral palsy, but that did not stop him from founding and operating a full-time, year-round facility for handicapped individuals. His influence has brought many to Christ and ministered to hundreds of handicapped individuals, giving them a home and community.

Joni Erickson Tada had a diving accident at age 16 that left her quadriplegic. But she had a keen mind and began speaking from her wheelchair. Billy Graham noticed this and featured her in a motion picture, making her famous. For years following, she had a daily radio broadcast and wrote several books.

What is your "problem?" What is your excuse for not using it as a platform to speak for God? It may be just a neighbor or co-worker. You may never become famous. But God doesn't reward fame; He rewards faithfulness. Our weaknesses are His springboard for greatness. Chris Tiegreen, devotional author, says, "Like Paul, we can do all things in Christ who strengthens us. (Phil 4:13) We have great strength, but it's not ours. We have amazing status, but we didn't earn it. We can be incredibly influential in matters of eternity, but only by the Spirit who works within us. The mind must be disciplined to know two extremes: our utter poverty of power and our indestructible position in Christ. When we focus on the former, we become helpless and impotent. When we focus on the latter, we become proud. But the balance will keep us humble and change our lives dramatically. Our weakness becomes God's opportunity to be strong."

Remember Paul's statement, "I am what I am by the grace of God." (I Cor. 15:10) (My paraphrase)

"WHAT'S IN YOUR HAND?"

I wrote a devotional asking what you are doing with the abilities you have. This response from a friend of over 50 years is worth sharing with all of you, with his permission.

"I've always enjoyed cooking but never thought much of it. In my late high school years, my single mom realized I had left home from school before she got home from work, so she left me instructions on how to make dinner. And many of my early jobs had me working in a kitchen. On one of our first dates, my then-girlfriend made dinner for us at her place. By that time in my life, the rule that whoever cooks doesn't clean was so ingrained that I didn't think twice about cleaning up and was shocked to be emphatically told never to go in the kitchen. Apparently, in my wife's family, that was 'momma's place,' and no one else was allowed. This meant the girl I eventually married had no experience in the kitchen (and was very intimidated by it), but she couldn't tolerate my being in the kitchen. Obviously, something had to change.

"About 12 years into our marriage, we had three children and a family crisis eventually led to me being a stay-at-home dad. It was not my plan, but it certainly put my cooking skills to work. By this point, my wife was happy I could cook and completely resigned to it. Truth be told, as much as I enjoy cooking, there was a side to me that felt very unmanly about the whole arrangement that I just never spoke about. It was just my own ongoing, internal 'pout.'

"At one point in our marriage, our teens were in high school, and we were praying the Lord would help us live out our faith so that our children would experience the Living God, not man's religion. Honestly, it took years in retrospect to realize that what ended up happening was likely an answer to that prayer. To be brief, we ended up taking on three 'foster children,' whose parents were incarcerated. We didn't know them, they didn't know us, and they were too young to understand what was happening. They were afraid and disoriented at ages 9, 6, and 2. I was making breakfast as I prayed the Lord would help me help them, and I remembered a lesson I heard Francis Schaeffer give, where God asked Moses, 'What's in your hand?' Moses said, 'A rod.' It was just his walking stick that Moses used as a shepherd (a career that was repulsive to his Egyptian-raised sensitivities). As Moses relinquished the seemingly mundane things to God, it became a powerful tool through which God used Moses to lead His people. So, as I stood at the stove, I sensed God asking me the same question, and it admittedly was with a great deal of sass and attitude that I answered the question, 'What's in your hand,' by saying, 'A spatula,' as if nothing could be so useless and so low. So began another lesson for me from my Master.

Taking this as a challenge, I began to use my cooking 'specialty' to reach those girls. Each meal had to be well presented, making the house smell good and touch their favorite flavors. Popcorn or fresh cookies when they came home, fresh bread before dinner, bacon or sausage in the morning, and on the list went. At one point, my wife overheard the 9-year-old talking on the phone to her mother when the young girl said, 'Mom, when you get out, we need to get a 'Dave.' Indeed, our time with those girls, and our children's time with them, continues, and my cooking remains a big part of that relationship (in which mother and children came to Christ.)

"After seminary, I interned at a large church outside Hartford, CT. At my one-year anniversary, I was in an Elder meeting, and the Pastor asked me, quite spontaneously, if I had observed anything about their church in my first year. I mentioned many complimentary things, then added that the large room underneath their sanctuary (with a sign over the door identifying it as 'Fellowship Hall) had not so much as had the lights on any Sunday for the previous year. They never used it, meaning they didn't fellowship. The pastor and elders gave many reasons for this, and what they had tried, concluding that their congregation just wasn't into that. Referring to Acts 2:42, I assured them that their congregation needed fellowship, and it was our job (as leaders) to lead them to it. I challenged them to give me a Sunday, and I would fill that room. The night before the designated Sunday, I drove the 1:20 minutes from my home to the church at 3 am and began making cinnamon buns from scratch. As the buns were rising, I opened all the interior doors to the church, putting fans to circulate the kitchen smell throughout the church. Eventually, coffee, hot cider, and other smells were added. When people started to arrive, I removed the fans and closed the doors. After the first service (they have three), the pastor announced what everyone else could already smell. For the next six months, we had a packed "Fellowship Hall" every Sunday, combining people from all three services as our menu expanded, and many congregants were happy to add to the banquet, leaving uncooked casseroles and items with instructions for me (or my then team) to cook on site. The only reason it stopped was Covid. And it is my understanding they have since re-continued the practice. That first Sunday, I knew I hit the target when an elderly lady poked her head in the kitchen to thank me and relay that she was sitting in the balcony, smelling the kitchen, listening to the sermon with her eyes closed, and feeling like she was home.

In this case, what I 'do' is not linked, per se, to my vocation. It is, however, linked to who I am. And the Lord has shown me, what we find in our hands (our specialization) may seem meaningless but becomes quite influential if we are willing to give it to him."—David R., Stamford, CT

So I ask **you**, what's in **your** hand? What could you possibly leverage as a tool to be a significant witness? For me, it is a computer. The day I retired, I barely knew how to turn one on. Twenty-four years and millions of words later, I still type with two fingers and two thumbs! I'm not very mobile, but my fingers work. I know people on this list probably do not know the Lord. I do not know that they read every devotional, but I often write with them in mind and trust that the Lord will speak to them. And, of course, I trust that if you think about it, they will also be meaningful to you.

I know a man who makes toy wooden cars and a woman who knits doilies for missionaries. Several men travel to the mission field to use their expertise in building construction and medicine. I know a group of people who collect used stamps and somehow turn them into money sent to the mission field. I see a woman who is an excellent cook who volunteers to go to various mission fields to cook when needed, as others are home on deputation.

I like David's statement, "In this case, what I 'do' is not linked, per se, to my vocation. It is, however, linked to who I am."

What can you do? What's in your hand? What is your expertise? What can be linked to you?

E. GOD USES IMPERFECT PEOPLE

When a person writes an autobiography, he/she tells the good parts of his/her life and talks very well about people who were meaningful in their lives. Or when we go to a funeral and ask people to say a word about the deceased, it is always good. (Imagine: he was a liar and a cheat. I'm glad he's out of here!) One of the many reasons I believe the Bible is the literal word of God is that it tells the truth about people, even the bad things about them. This gives me hope because you and I know we are not perfect.

God is not looking for perfect people, he is looking for people who have a heart for him, who have a strong desire to serve him in spite of their weaknesses. God uses imperfect people.

- Jacob was a cheater (he deceived Esau twice and cheated him out of his birthright)
- Peter denied his relationship with Jesus (with a servant girl)
- David had an affair (Bathsheba)
- Noah got drunk (went to bed with two daughters-in-law)
- Jonah ran from God (great fish)
- Paul was a murderer (stoned Christians)
- Gideon was insecure (he wanted a sign from God before he would act)
- Martha was a worrier (worried about getting a meal instead of sitting at Jesus' feet)
- Thomas was a doubter (until I see the nail prints in his hands)
- Sarah was impatient (she gave a handmaid to have a son when God had promised one to her through Abraham)
- Elijah was depressed (sat under the juniper tree and fled from Ahab and Jezebel)
- Moses stuttered (Aaron spoke for him)
- Zaccheus was short (not impressive as a man)
- Abraham lied (twice about his wife, saying she was his sister)

- Lazarus was dead (an example of the miracle-working ability of the Lord)
- the disciples were uneducated fishermen and a tax collector (and they changed the known world)
- And God chose a tiny nation, Israel, about the size of New Jersey, to bring about the Messiah.

God doesn't call the qualified, He qualifies the CALLED! Sometimes very ordinary people turn out to be very extra-ordinary when they turn their lives over to Christ.

God even uses hypocrites!

I'm a hypocrite! Are you? A hypocrite is someone who says one thing and does another. The dictionary says, "a feigning to believe what one is not."

- I hope you think I am nice, but sometimes I am very nasty!
- I tell you to hold your tongue, and I spout off with mine.
- I want you to be patient with me, but I am not very patient with you.

And I haven't told you the nasty stuff! If you really knew me, especially my past, you'd not listen to a word I have to say.

But don't get uppity. You're probably just as guilty as I am.

The great Apostle Paul described this inner conflict: "For I do not understand my own actions. For I do not do what I want, but I do the very thing I hate." If he had a problem, imagine me!

Look how God used him!!!

Jesus hated hypocrisy. He said, "The teachers of the law and the Pharisees sit in Moses' seat. So, you must be careful to do everything they tell you. But do not do what they do, for they do not practice what they preach."—Matthew 23:1-3 They say one thing but do another. They were notorious hypocrites.

But what about that sin you can't seem to shake: your besetting sin, the sin that so easily entangles you? We all have one, if we're honest.

There is a crippling sin suited explicitly for every personality. Generally, it appears as a "friend" coming to satisfy a need or a craving. Good people rarely wake up one morning saying, "I think I'll sin against God today." Sin creeps in where it sees a hurt, a sense of inferiority, pompous pride, or an unmet craving. It comes promising to satisfy.

The moment you surrender, however, you are cast under its power. Like a slave master, the sin demands submission. Each time you cry for mercy, God grants it. Then the slave master beats you until you return to the sin, and the cycle of guilt and repentance starts all over again.

No support comes from our degenerating civilization. Society approves of what you know to be sin. Spiritually corrupt leaders lacking solutions then legalize it. Yet, what brought brief delight has now turned destructive. You know what is right but feel powerless to do it.

Neither you nor I can break the power of sin without heaven-sent help. If we could, then Jesus died in vain. In his death, however, he broke the power of sin. He always grants His power to all who wholeheartedly seek His Father.

But God uses imperfect, ordinary people. People like you and me.

How has God gifted you?

As a 38-year-old housewife, she would go to the movies and sigh, "If only I had her looks." She would listen to a singer and moan, "If only I had her voice." Then, one day, someone gave her a copy of "The Magic of Believing." She stopped comparing herself with actresses and singers. She stopped crying about what she didn't have and started concentrating on what she did have. She took inventory of herself and remembered that in high school, she had a reputation for being the funniest girl around. She began to turn her liabilities into assets. When she was at the top of her career, Phyllis Diller made over $1,000,000 a year. She wasn't good-looking, and she had a scratchy voice; but she could make people laugh.

Where is your heart? What could you do at your age and with your skills that would give you tremendous fulfillment? What are you doing for Jesus? What could you do for Jesus? How will people remember you?

Mary Esther and I attended a funeral several years ago where people were allowed to say something about the deceased. Almost everyone remembered him as a great drinking buddy who could hold his liquor. We were at another where the most mentioned issue was his love of playing bridge. Both of these were regular church attendees. This was a stark reminder that you can go to church faithfully and yet not be remembered as someone who loved Jesus and wanted to be a witness for him.

I'm so glad God uses imperfect, ordinary people. I'm happy that I'm a part of the "anything" God can use. If I have my desire, when I am lying in that coffin, and people speak about me, I know some will talk about my love of fishing, and others will talk about me being a musician, but what I want is for people to recognize that I wanted my life to please the Lord. I don't want to be known as a person who preached one thing and lived another.

How do you want to be remembered? What will you do for God?

After considering what you have read so far, are you in agreement? Has it caused you to investigate further? I trust many practical issues have stirred your thoughts and perhaps even changed your life.

5

END TIMES

There is much talk these days about a massive change in the world as we know it. Some see it as a result of a war or many smaller wars. Some see it as predicted in the Bible. Almost everyone acknowledges that something must be done, or we are doomed.

The Bible has much to say, but many do not believe it. On the other hand, much of what the Bible predicts has been fulfilled exactly as prophesied in the first millennium. That which remains unfulfilled is a part of our daily news.

I want to unwrap this subject for you. I must use the Bible. There is so much discussion and interpretation on this issue that I must go into great detail to cover the subject faithfully.

We are talking about prophecy. In the Old Testament, a prophet would be stoned if his prophecy was not fulfilled. (Of course, many of them died because their prophecies extended to the far future.)

More than 300 prophecies were minutely fulfilled in the coming of Christ as the Messiah, a baby born precisely as predicted centuries before the actual birth. It is important to note that each condition (prophecy) was minutely fulfilled.

Likewise, hundreds of prophecies speak of a second coming of Christ. There is little debate about that. The discussion has to do with the timing and conditions of His return, not with whether or not He will return.

SECTION ONE

A. PROPHETIC SIGNIFICANCE

1. Israel

Many Old Testament prophecies concern Israel's nation and land. Many relate to God's plans for the nation, warnings of judgment because of their disobedience, and restoration after the Assyrians and the Babylonians conquered them.

There are also comforting prophecies about Israel's distant future, especially their role in the future righteous kingdom that the Messiah will establish.

In our lifetime, we have witnessed one of the most amazing fulfillments—the promise of Ezekiel chapters 36 and 37 that the chosen people will be brought back from all over the earth and re-born as a nation. Of course, this was fulfilled in 1948 when, against all odds, Israel declared independence. With God's help, it has fought off enemies on all sides for over 65 years.

The current wave of violence between Israel and the Palestinians could die out and become one of many such cycles in the area, or it could lead to a more serious war, such as the one predicted in Psalm 83. The outcome of this war could be a welcome peace agreement.

Such a peace agreement might be just another phase in the age-old struggle between the descendants of Isaac and Ishmael, or it could be a present false peace mentioned in 1 Thessalonians 5:3. While people are saying, "Peace and safety, destruction will come on them suddenly, as labor pains on a pregnant woman, and they will not escape."

When Israel finally is at peace, it will be the first time since it became a nation in 1948 that it has enjoyed such security. This could cause them to lower their guard, setting the scene for the War of Gog and Magog predicted in Ezekiel 38 and 39. This war will most likely correspond to the 2nd Seal of Revelation 6. A dramatic end of this great war of the 2nd seal could produce the treaty predicted in Daniel 9:27, which many prophecy scholars identify as the beginning of Israel and the Church. What are the differences?

2. The Church

One of the great theological battlegrounds of orthodox Christianity throughout the centuries has been the nature and character of the Church, especially to its biblical predecessor, Israel. The two major views are that:

A. First View: The Church is a continuation of Israel

The predominant view has been that the Church is the "new" Israel, a continuation of the concept of Israel, which began in the Old Testament. In this view, the Church is the refinement and higher development of the idea of Israel. All the promises made to Israel in the Scriptures find their fulfillment in the Church. Thus, the prophecies relating to the blessing and restoration of Israel to the Promised Land are "spiritualized" into promises of blessing to the Church. The prophecies of condemnation and judgment are retained literally by the Jewish nation of Israel.

This view is sometimes called Replacement Theology because the Church is seen to replace Israel in God's economy. One of the problems with the view, among others, is the continuing existence of the Jewish people, especially concerning the revival of the new modern state of Israel. Suppose Israel has been condemned to extinction, and there is no divinely ordained future for the Jewish nation. How then does one account for the supernatural survival of the Jewish people since the establishment of the Church, for almost 2,000 years against all odds? Furthermore, how does one account for Israel's resurgence among the family of nations as an independent nation, victorious in several wars and flourishing economically?

B. Second View: The Church is completely different from Israel

(This article is scheduled to appear in the Dictionary of Premillennial Theology and be published by Kregel Publications. It has been significantly shortened, retaining the crucial elements to cover the subject.)

"The other view, pre-millennialists believe, is clearly taught in the New Testament, but it has been suppressed throughout most of Church history. This view is that the Church is entirely different and distinct from Israel, and the two should not be confused. In fact, the Church is an entirely new creation that came into being on the Day of Pentecost after Christ's resurrection from the dead and will continue until it is taken to Heaven at return of the Lord (Eph. 1:9-11). None of the curses or blessings pronounced upon Israel refer directly to the Church. The Church enters into the Abrahamic and New Covenants, for instance, only by divine application, not by original interpretation. (Matt 26:28).

"This leaves all the covenants, promises, and warnings to Israel intact. Israel, the natural Jewish nation, is still Israel.

"Not only has God preserved the Jewish nation, but He has also kept His promise to save a remnant of Israel in every generation. The remnant of Israel in this age is the Jewish believers in Christ who have joined the Gentile believers and formed the Church, the Body of Christ (Rom. 11:5).

"In the future, God's warnings and promises to Israel will pass after the Lord finishes the Church Age and takes the Church to Heaven (1 Thess. 4:16-18); God will restore Israel to center stage on the world's divine theater.

"When Christ does return to the earth, Israel will be ready, willing, and eager to receive Him and proclaim, "Blessed is He who comes in the name of the Lord" (Matt. 23:39).

"While the Jewish nation still has a dark period facing it, there is a glorious finale to Israel's long history."

3. How Did the Church Decide the Demise of Israel?

"Many Jewish believers were not comfortable with the Gentile believers at first, but as time went on and Gentiles began to predominate numerically, the attitudes reversed. Galatians shows how the Jewish party tried to impose the Mosaic Law on Gentile Christians, and Romans shows how the Gentile party began to 'consider yourself to be superior to those other branches' (Rom. 11:18), resenting the place of Israel in history and theology.

"It took some time, perhaps a couple of centuries, but eventually, the vast Gentile majority in the Church began to view Israel as a vestigial organ that had outlived its usefulness. If there was any purpose for the existence of the Jewish people, it was to remind the world of the severe judgment of God upon a disobedient people.

"If this harsh view of Israel were accurate, though, what of the promises of God to Israel in the Old Testament? For those who claimed to believe in the entire Bible as the Word of God, this was a significant problem. How could a faithful God not keep His promises to His ancient people? To deal with this took extraordinary theological dexterity and alchemy. The theologians had to propose that Israel in the Scriptures did not really mean Israel, especially when it came to the promises of eternal blessing. Instead, Israel meant something else that came to be known in the New Testament as the Church. The Church became the new Israel, and through this remarkable transformation, wherever a blessing is promised to Israel in the Old Testament, it was interpreted to mean the Church. This is Replacement Theology, in which the Church has become Israel."

Only during the last Century or so has the Premillennial concept of the future of Israel come to the forefront in evangelical Christianity. Even so, it is a minority view.

4. Does Israel's Future Demean the Church's Glory?

"Some suggest that if Israel has not ceased to exist in its covenant relationship with God and if Israel still has a future in the divine plan, this somehow diminishes the position of the Church. Is such a concern valid? "It is when the Church recognizes Israel that the true distinctiveness and glory of the Body of Christ becomes evident. This called-out body, composed of believing Jews and Gentiles during the Church Age, is the highest entity the Lord has created, superior to the universe, all the Angels, the nations, and Israel.

"Why be jealous of the future destiny of Israel? How short-sighted of us! Indeed, the Church's finest and most distinctive hour will be when Israel is restored nationally and spiritually to the Lord at the Second Coming of Christ. We will return from Heaven with Him as His glorious Bride to rule Israel and the world. What more could we ask?

"So, if we are not to suffer from spiritual myopia, we must recognize what the Lord is doing with Israel, not shrink from it as though our own interests will be overshadowed. Instead, we rejoice in these developments, with full assurance that our own redemption draws ever closer."

SECTION TWO

Eschatological Definitions

Without becoming too detailed, there are four words that are necessary to understand:

1. Millennium. This is a period in which Jesus will come to rule the earth along with those who have accepted Him as Savior throughout the ages. It is 1000 years long and will be characterized by total peace between man and beasts. Satan will be bound and will have no evil influence. Towards the end, man will again turn evil, and Christ will return as the earth's ruler. Here is the Bible passage: Rev 20: 1-3.
2. Rapture. This is a sudden, secret return of Christ to snatch away those who are alive and are believers and to resurrect the dead who were believers during their lives. They refer to these verses: I Cor. 15:51-57; Thess. 4:13-18.
3. Tribulation Period. This is seven years during which the earth will experience total turmoil. This turmoil will culminate in the Battle of Armageddon, which will wipe out more than two-thirds of the world's population. Even the stars and universe will be shaken. They cite these verses: Daniel 9:24-27, Rev. 11:2-3 and 13:5.
4. Second Coming. (Also called "The Return of Christ.") This is the climatic event when Christ binds Satan and his angels (demons) and casts them into hell...the second death. Now, all believers spend all eternity with Christ in heaven, and all non-believers spend all of eternity in hell, a place of never-ending torment. (Luke 21:34-36; Acts 1:11; I Thess. 4:13-18; Titus 2:13; II Peter 3:8-14; I John 3:2-3.)

I want to state very clearly that much of the following is taken directly from other writers. Authors practice significant research when writing. I have researched this subject for many years and compiled notes from various sources, all of which I have not noted appropriately. I have not attempted to plagiarize, though some of this is exactly or close to what I researched. This is my disclaimer.

A vital resource for me is "The Meaning of the Millennium," edited by Robert G. Clouse. Four scholars present their views in it, and then the other three dissect them. Here are the differences in interpretation gained from this book. It all centers around the Millennium:

A. The premillennial position
   1. Pre-millennialists believe that Christ is coming before the millennium.

2. This is the rapture. Christ will snatch away His own before this terrible seven-year turmoil known as "The Great Tribulation." According to this position, the believers will not go through the tribulation.

3. Mid-tribulation position. The rapture occurs in the middle of the seven years so that Christ's followers will not suffer through the worst part of the tribulation.

4. Post-tribulation position. The rapture takes place after the tribulation. Believers must go through the entire tribulation.

All three positions believe in a secret snatching away (the rapture) but believe the second coming of Christ is in two stages: the rapture and the visible second seven years later.

B. Amillennialists believe there is no literal millennium. The thousand-year period is symbolic, and when Christ returns, He rules and reigns. Period.

C. Post-millennialists believe that Christ will come after the millennium. There is no such thing as the rapture. The second coming is a one-time event.

Each of those positions had their day. Premillennialism was the dominant interpretation during the first three centuries of the Christian era. During the Middle Ages, amillennialism prevailed. Martin Luther and Charles Wesley began a change in thinking, which turned people back to premillennialism. But postmillennialism then asserted itself (1638-1726). Then, in 1800-1882, Charles Darby proposed a new kind of premillennialism, dispensational premillennialism. The President of Dallas Theological Seminary, Dr.Walvoord, championed this view; today, it is probably the leading interpretation. (Thus, there is historic and dispensational premillennialism.)

I want to discuss the dispensational premillennial position, which I was taught and believed (with questions) for my entire life until I retired when I studied and slightly modified it.

In this theological position, there is the rapture, followed by the Great Tribulation and then Christ's second coming. Note that sequence. Following that second coming, there is the one-thousand-year millennium when Christ reigns on earth, and there is peace.

B. DISPENSATIONALIST INTERPRETATION OF SCRIPTURE

Dispensationalists have as a cardinal rule for scriptural interpretation, "when the plain sense of Scripture makes common sense, seek no other sense; therefore, take every word at its primary, ordinary, usual, literal meaning?" Some would add, "...unless the facts of the immediate context, studied in the light of related passages and axiomatic and fundamental truths, indicate clearly otherwise." *This is critical to understand and consistently apply.* I submit to you that many of the above scriptures, especially Daniel 9:24, upon which most of the others stand or fall, do not come close to following the guidelines for their interpretation.

Even more interesting if you read precisely what the text says without trying to force another thought pattern into it is that Jesus said this would happen "in a little while": they (the apostles) would experience it; there is not a 2000-year gap! See Matt. 14:18-19; 14:28; 16:16-22 (think about the whole passage and how it unfolds).

C. JUST ONE VERSE

Is it a fair statement to make that most, if not all, major doctrines of the Bible can be cited in one verse or brief passage? There may be more than one, but at least there is one that states it clearly. Is there just one verse or brief passage for each of the following that specifically and unmistakably teaches:

1. That there is a gap in the 490 years (70 weeks) of Daniel 9:24 and the last seven years are yet to come;
2. That there is a seven-year tribulation and an antichrist foretold in Daniel 9:26-27;
3. That the Second Coming is split into two events;
4. That the rapture occurs seven years before the revelation of Christ;
5. That the rapture is secretive and as sudden as the blink of an eye;
6. That those who are raptured are taken to heaven;
7. That the 144,000 of Revelation chapter seven are future Jewish evangelists;
8. That the "great tribulation" is described in Revelation chapters six, seven or eight to nineteen;
9. That the first resurrection occurs in two phases seven years apart.

Jack VanImpe, John Hagee, Hal Lindsey, Tim LaHaye, Grant Jeffrey, Dave Breese, and many others have **in print** that we (you and I) are the terminal generation, more easily stated that we would not see the year 2000. Well, here we are 25 years later! Didn't these Bible scholars know that the word used for "generation" in the passage to which they refer was also used for family, children at play (Matt 11:16-19), men who seek signs (Matt 12:

39-42), men who reject Christ (Luke 17:25), men who kill the prophets and righteous (Matt 23 29-36)? Obviously, it was not a generation that began after 1968, when Israel became a nation again. We are now more than 50 years past that date.

D. THE RAPTURE

Pre-Millennial Dispensationalists believe the rapture, a secret snatching away of the saints alive at the time, will come just before the Great Tribulation. This means that "the church," all true believers, will not suffer the agonies of the tribulation. Here is where I part company with this group. And here is why:

1. In Daniel chapters 9 and 12, we have a prophecy establishing a timeline for future events. It is "seventy times seven weeks" (490) and in chapter 12 it reads, "From the time that the daily sacrifice is abolished and the abomination that causes desolation is set up, there will be 1,290 days. Blessed is the one who waits for and reaches the end of the 1,335 days."
2. Pre-tribulation theology says there is an undetermined gap between weeks sixty-nine and seventy. Remember how Pre-tribers are to read the Bible...interpret it literally if it makes sense. Is this clear passage clear? Does it make sense? They must have a gap, or the entire system is invalid. They invented the gap.
3. The Bible never mentions a pre-tribulation rapture. It uses analogies to demonstrate it, such as Noah being taken out before the flood, but there is never a direct reference to Christians being taken out before a tribulation.
4. It is not taught in church history. It was first conceived by Margaret McDonald in 1827 in a dream and picked up by John Darby in 1850, who developed it. C.I. Scofield adopted and popularized it in his Scofield Reference Bible and many accompanying writings. Scofield was instrumental in Dallas Theological Seminary, which trained hundreds of pastors and spread it widely across the USA. Later, Hal Lindsey's book, "Late Great Planet Earth," was widely popular, and the "Left Behind Series" of books and motion pictures put it in the mainstream. All of them were wrong, as were their ardent disciples! Some were very precise and dogmatic, and when the predictions did not come through, it set back the believability of the Christian message to minds already skeptical or open.
5. You will not find it widely taught in countries not influenced by American conservative teaching. That's another way of saying that it must be taught. There

is no conceivable way that a person reading the Bible on his own, even over a long period, could concoct this doctrine.

E. PERTINENT SCRIPTURES CONCERNING CHRIST'S RETURN

1. In the Twinkling of an Eye: Pre-tribbers talk about being secretly snatched away in the twinkling of an eye (I Cor 15:51-52)! Anyone who can read and understand English can read that we are "changed" in the twinkling of an eye, not snatched away! I John 3:1-2 clearly states, "When Christ appears, we shall be like him." What happens? "The spiritual body will become imperishable and immortal at the last trumpet!" When does this happen? At the last trumpet, the seventh trumpet. And when is that? Rev 11:15 when "the kingdom of the world has become the kingdom of our Lord…and he shall reign forever and ever." That is not at the so-called rapture of I Thess 4.

2. Even the Elect Can Be Mislead
   a. Now if there are three or four major doctrines on the second coming, and all are espoused by true believers (the elect), only one can be correct. And that's precisely what Jesus said (Matthew 24:34). If it could happen in the days of the apostles, it can happen today. Many are clearly misled! All of us cannot be correct!

3. The Holy Spirit is Gone
   a. We have been taught that Satan is loosed to deceive the nations because the Holy Spirit is "taken out of the way" or removed. A respected friend and great Bible teacher said something different. I sent him a note: "I was quite surprised by your very quick comment in the "Armageddon" session that he (the Holy Spirit) releases Satan to do his work of deception but is still present to convict and convert (or something close to that…it went by so quickly that I missed the exact quote). I never heard that before! Not in 50 years of listening to prophecy messages! The text says "he (the Holy Spirit, apparently) is taken out of the way" (II Thess 2:7). Whatever your precise quote was, I remember thinking, where did he find that? Is there another verse you were referring to?"
   b. We believe a part of the work of the Holy Spirit is to move upon the hearts and consciences of man, affording light and influence to convict them of sin, regenerate and dwell in them (Acts 2:17; John 16:8-11; I Cor 2:4). If he is taken

<u>out</u> of the way, how can he convict men of sin who will be saved during the Great Tribulation?

4. Petra (Matt.24:15-21)

   a. "So when you see standing in the holy place 'the abomination that causes desolation,' spoken of through the prophet Daniel—let the reader understand—<u>then let those who are in Judea flee to the mountains.</u> Let no one on the housetop go down to take anything out of the house. Let no one in the field go back to get their cloak. <u>How dreadful it will be in those days for pregnant women and nursing mothers! Pray that your flight will not take place in winter or on the Sabbath.</u> For then there will be great distress, unequaled from the beginning of the world until now—and never to be equaled again." (<u>My underline.</u>)

   b. We were always taught that "flee to the mountains" indicated fleeing to Petra, a "city" in the mountains with only one very narrow entrance/exit. We've been there. The point is that it is easily secured.

   c. This made great sense in Bible times, but today, one bomb or rocket could destroy the whole "city." This alone makes the passage questionable in the way dispensationalists interpret it.

5. "Then the End (of the Temple) Will Come" Vss. 14-20

   a. When all the events listed in verses 5-14 come to pass, *"then the end will come."* The end of what? It cannot be the end of the age, though that quickly comes to mind because of the secondary question (Mt. 24:3) asked by the disciples. It cannot refer to that end because all the events listed were fulfilled in the apostles' lifetimes.

F. IMMINENCE

This word does not appear in the Bible, but its meaning began when Christ descended into heaven. He told His disciples He would return and that they were to watch for Him. In other words, they expected Him to return in their lifetimes. Imminence means nearness, soon. For the past two millennia, people have expected Christ to return. Back in 1970, it began to be used very frequently. Jesus is coming soon. Through the years, many have done strange things awaiting Him.

Throughout Church history, people have often been wrong about Christ's return. Many were convinced that Jesus would come in A.D. 1000, so they sold everything, went to Jerusalem, and waited. And waited. Nothing happened.

Others sold everything they had and waited for Christ to return to America in the 1840s. And waited. Nothing. The Seventh-day Adventist denomination was born out of that experience.

When Hitler was alive, some people thought he was the Anti-Christ. Can you blame them?

Through the ages, even otherwise, servants of Christ have mistakenly predicted a specific date of the end of the world. This category includes Christopher Columbus, Sir Isaac Newton, and Cotton Mather.

I even read one such prophet who essentially said—with a straight face—that Christ didn't tell us the day or the hour of His return, but that doesn't mean we can't know the year, the month, or the week!

It's tragic to me that the watching world looks at such predictions that come and go and laugh, justifiably so, at those who think Christ will return one day.

I am as sure of Jesus Christ's return to planet earth someday as I am that the sun will rise tomorrow.

The group that made the May 21, 2011, prediction says this: "The Bible has opened up its secrets concerning the timeline of history. This information was never previously known because God had closed up His Word, blocking any attempt to gain knowledge of the end of the world."

But now *they* know, supposedly.

A friend of mine noted this is like modern-day Gnosticism.

The Gnostics were an early Church heresy that got the basics of the faith wrong. They claimed that the way of salvation was not Christ crucified, for sinners died and raised from the dead, but rather some sort of *secret knowledge.*

The founder of Calvary Chapel, Chuck Smith, predicted that the generation of 1948 would be the last and that the world would end by 1981. Smith acknowledged that he "could be wrong" but continued to say in the same sentence that his prediction was "a deep conviction in my heart, and all my plans are predicated upon that belief."

In the 1970s, half of the speakers at Sandy Cove preached on the imminent return. By that, they meant any day and very soon in our lifetime. I have sat at a dining table with nationally known Bible teachers who had it all figured out. That summer at the Bible Conference in 1971, all twenty speakers gave at least one message on Christ's return. Some gave all of their messages on that subject. The decade of the 70s and 80s was on fire for the return of Christ. John W. Peterson wrote his beloved cantata "Jesus is Coming" (which I had the privilege of doing with him in seven cities), and we sang dozens of songs explicitly dedicated to that theme. Best-selling albums by Christian artists all featured "big" selections on it. I love those songs.

In my early lifetime and memory, the second coming was not a primary emphasis in our churches. Then Hal Lindsey wrote "The Late Great Planet Earth." It was just as I left for a month's ministry in Ecuador in 1970. I knew I would have much time alone and wanted something to read. This book changed my life. I had never heard these things before; they all came straight from the Bible. (I only heard of it but never knew of other options.) I was hooked. I read it twice and underlined many passages.

Hal Lindsey wrote in "The Late Great Planet Earth," interpreted as Jesus coming sometime before 1984 or possibly 1988. Harold Camping gave specific dates in September twice, a year apart, because he missed it the first time. The second, too! (Incidentally, he was in our auditorium preaching the predicted date to come in September while a staff member was in our sales office negotiating a contract for the next June!) He died humiliated. But here we are. Jerry Falwell said it would be within ten years of his lifetime. In the '70s and early '80s, a series of books sold millions of copies, the "Left Behind" series. Ed Dobson predicted 2000. There was Y2K, which was to be the end. Jack Van Impe gave several dates and finally stopped after 2012. They were wrong. We're still here. All of them knew the scripture, "But about that day or hour (Christ's return) no one knows, not even the angels in heaven, nor the Son, but only the Father."

It has been my experience in the past 10-20 years that one of the missing subjects in preaching is the return of Christ. Is this a "time when we think not?" (Matt 24:44) Which of the two extremes is most correct?

I have noted that many former pre-trib diehards have changed their minds or avoided the subject. They've been wrong too many times!

But what about now? With one exception, I have not heard a message <u>dedicated explicitly</u> to the second coming in years. In contemporary churches, I am aware that few, if any, songs are specifically focused on this event. (My children and grandchildren are vitally involved.)

I am again reminded of the scripture, "and many false prophets will appear and deceive many people. Because of the increase of wickedness, the love of most will grow cold, but the one who stands firm to the end will be saved." (Matt. 24:11-13.) Or the ten virgins who were not prepared for the coming of the bridegroom. (Matt 25:1-13). II Peter 2 gives us two insights in this regard. Verse 3 says, "Knowing this first, that there shall come in the last days scoffers, walking after their own lusts, and saying, 'Where is the promise of his coming? for since the fathers fell asleep, all things continue as they were from the beginning of the creation.'" And verse 10, "But the day of the Lord will come as a thief in the night; in the which the heavens shall pass away with a great noise, and the elements shall melt with fervent heat, the earth also and the works that are therein shall be burned up." (KJV)

In these days, we need to remember His return, but we have been focused on our own pleasures, our own worship styles, and meeting our own needs. We have been led astray, not by false teaching but by a lack of teaching, and many will surely be surprised, as the thief in the night surprises us.

Regardless of the theological debate and positioning, many Christians really do care to have it all wrapped up in a nice package. They plead, "He is coming." We all agree. But no one knows for certain exactly when that will be. Thus, the main, vital issue is to be ready.

But I have no idea when, and I will not engage in speculation based on "jigsaw theology."

Prophecy is history being revealed before it happens. This speaks specifically of Israel:

In A.D. 70, the Jews were scattered among the world's nations. After nearly 1900 years, the Jews returned to their homeland, and the rebirth of Israel as a nation took place in 1948. This is one of the greatest fulfillments of Bible prophecy. On 5/14/48, the nation was regathered and reborn.

The scriptural basis for this is Ezekiel 37:1-14, written in the 6th century BC, especially verses 12-14: "Therefore prophesy and say to them: this is what the Sovereign Lord says: 'O my people, I am going to open your graves and bring you up from them; I will bring you back to the land of Israel. Then you, my people, will know that I am the Lord, when I open your graves and bring you up from them.'"

Someday Israel will experience a spiritual rebirth according to Ezekiel 36:25-33; Zechariah 12:10; 13:1; Ezekiel 39:27-29; Acts 2:17-18; Ezek. 37:14; Matt 24:44; Luke 24:47.

There are 5.6M Jews in Israel today. They have 300M enemies surrounding them but continue to win all wars against them!

Do you see the hand of God at work in fulfilling Bible prophecy? Do you believe God keeps His Word? Are you struggling to believe and obey God's promises?

Surrender to His Word and His way for your life.

G. NOT THE TIME OF JESUS' RETURN MATT 24: 23-27

Preterists believe and teach that in the AD 70 destruction of Jerusalem and the past tribulation of Israel Jesus fulfilled His promises to return again. In other words, that was the second coming.

Pretribulationalists believe and teach that Jesus will partially fulfill His promise to return before a future world tribulation.

Foreseeing that men would mistakenly believe and promote such ideas, Jesus made it very clear that He would not return at the time of Jerusalem's destruction or prior to the tribulation. He said that those who teach that are false Christs and false prophets who mislead even the elect. His stern admonition was, *"do not believe them."*

The point of verses 23 to 27 is stated in the 27th verse— His coming will be universally seen (Mt. 24:27, 30 & Rev. 1:7) and will be preceded by visible signs in the sky and on the earth (Joel 2:30; Mt. 24:29; Rev. 6:12-17). These signs and His coming will occur after those days' tribulation. (Mt. 24:29).

H. THE EASTERN GATE CLOSED UNTIL MESSIAH RETURNS

According to the Bible, the Messiah would come, pass through the Eastern Gate, present Himself officially as King, be rejected by the Jews, and then close the Eastern Gate until he returned and was accepted by the Jews.

This Eastern Gate is closed today for over a thousand years despite several attempts to reopen it.

There are eight major gates to the Old City. The first and most important one is the Golden Gate, or the Eastern Gate, the only external gate that gives access to the Temple Mount.

The Eastern Gate has a remarkable story. God gave Ezekiel a supernatural vision of this gate, and it is a remarkable story.

Ezekial 43:1 "Afterward he brought me to the gate, the gate that faces toward the east. And behold, the glory of the God of Israel came from the way of the east".

Ezekial 43:4; "And the glory of the Lord came into the temple by the way of the gate which faces toward the east."

Ezekiel 44:1-3 "Then He brought me back to the outer gate which faces toward the east, but it was shut. And the Lord said to me, This gate shall be shut; it shall not be opened, and no man shall enter by it, because the Lord God of Israel has entered by it; therefore it shall be shut."

Proof that the Eastern Gate is built on the very spot it has always been was found. In 1969, Jerusalem archeologist James Fleming investigated the eastern wall of the temple, where a Muslim cemetery has long been located. It had rained heavily the night before, and the ground remained soggy the next day. As he investigated the area immediately in front of the Golden Gate, the ground beneath his feet gave way, and he dropped into a hole about eight feet deep. Fleming found himself "knee-deep in bones" and became suddenly aware he had fallen into a mass burial site. To him, the most amazing aspect of this incident was his clear view of five large wedge-shaped stones set into a massive arch. It appeared he had discovered an ancient gate under the present Golden Gate: "Then I noticed with astonishment that on the eastern face of the turret wall, directly beneath the Golden Gate itself, were five wedge-shaped stones neatly set in a massive arch spanning the turret wall. Here were the remains of an earlier gate to Jerusalem, below the Golden Gate, one that apparently had never been fully documented." (BAR, Jan./Feb. 1983, p30)

Matthew 21:1-5 "As they approached Jerusalem and came to Bethphage on the Mount of Olives, Jesus sent two disciples, saying to them, 'Go to the village ahead of you, and at once you will find a donkey tied there, with her colt by her. Untie them and bring them to me. If anyone says anything to you, say that the Lord needs them, and he will send them right away.' This took place to fulfill what was spoken through the prophet: Say to Daughter Zion, "See, your king comes to you, gentle and riding on a donkey, and on a colt, the foal of a donkey."'"

Daniel had predicted this very day would happen. Daniel 9:25: "Know therefore and understand, that from the going forth of the command to restore and build Jerusalem until Messiah the Prince, there shall be seven weeks and sixty-two weeks; the street shall be built again, and the wall, even in troublesome times."

Sixty-nine weeks is the Jewish way of saying 483 years.

According to this prophecy, a decree would be issued allowing the Jews to rebuild the wall. Several decrees were issued concerning the rebuilding of Jerusalem after the captivity, but only one concerned the wall. Artaxerxes issued this decree and is one of the best-known dates in history.

Sir Robert Anderson and Dr. Harold Hoehne have meticulously studied this prophecy, and both conclude that it was fulfilled on the very day Jesus entered Jerusalem through the Eastern Gate in His Triumphal Entry, 483 years to the day after the decree was made.

Now watch what Jesus told the Jews who rejected him.

"As he approached Jerusalem and saw the city, he wept over it and said, 'If you, even you, had only known on this day what would bring you peace—but now it is hidden from your eyes. They will dash you to the ground, you and the children within your walls. They will not leave one stone on another, because you did not recognize the time of God's coming to you.'" (Luke 19:41-42, 44).

If they had only kept up with the days predicted by Daniel, they would have known that this was the very day of its fulfillment. Jesus, having entered the city, said that he would not be seen again until Jerusalem acknowledged him. (Matthew 23:37-39)

1. Attempts to Open It

In the Six-Day War, some members of the Jewish military suggested catching the Jordanian defenders of the city off guard by blowing open the sealed Eastern Gate. But the leader of the group, an Orthodox Jew, had vehemently protested the idea, stating that "the Eastern Gate can be opened only when the Messiah comes."

In 1917, Muslim leaders in control of Jerusalem tried and failed to break the prophecy and open the gate. On the exact day, the workmen were preparing to demolish the ancient stone, the hand of God intervened, and the city of Jerusalem passed out of Muslim control into the hands of the British.

2. Why It Was Closed?

Jewish rabbis describe the Messiah as a great military leader who God would send from the east. He would enter the Eastern Gate and liberate the city from foreign control. To prevent this, the Muslims sealed the gate and put a Muslim cemetery in front of it, believing that a holy man would not defile himself by walking through a Muslim cemetery. Little did they know, they were fulfilling prophecy by doing this.

3. When Jesus returns, He will go through this gate again.

Acts 1:10-12 "They were looking intently up into the sky as he was going, when suddenly two men dressed in white stood beside them. 'Men of Galilee,' they said, 'why do you stand here looking into the sky? This same Jesus, who has been taken from you into heaven, will come back in the same way you have seen him go into heaven'".

Zechariah 14: 3,4: "Then the Lord will go forth and fight against those nations, as He fights in the day of battle. And on that day, His feet will stand on the Mount of Olives, which faces Jerusalem on the east. And the Mount of Olives shall split in two, from east to west, making a huge valley; half of the mountain shall move toward the north and half of it toward the south." Now, when did "The Lord" God have feet? When He comes the second time. The Mount of Olives faces the Eastern Gate, which his arrival will open.

In Isaiah 61 we are told that He will come from the east, and in Zechariah 14 we are told that He will touch ground on the Mount of Olives.

The eastern gate is especially holy for Jews, who believe that the Sheckinah, or Divine Presence, used to appear through it and will appear again. In the meantime, it is believed to be left untouched.

Some today suggest that this gate should be reopened to provide pilgrims greater access to the Temple Mount. Let's see how far they will get with their plans.

So, it appears that the Eastern Gate will remain closed, and when the Lord returns, this Psalm will be fulfilled. Psalm 24:7 says, "Lift up your heads, O gates, and be lifted up, O ancient doors, that the King of glory may come in! Who is the King of glory? The Lord strong and mighty, the Lord mighty in battle." Mike Clinton, June 23, 2013, Hiawassee Ga. Sources: Dr. David Reagan, Darrell G. Young, Lambert Dolphin, Walid Shoebat and others.

I. JESUS FORETELLS THE GREAT TRIBULATION OF ISRAEL IN MATTHEW 24:1-28 (KJV)

Chapter 24 of Matthew is one of the Bible's most abused and misused chapters. Many seem to be blinded by what is obvious in this chapter as they succumb to the ever-present danger of forcing a predetermined viewpoint upon the text rather than letting it tell its intended story. Of primary importance for a correct interpretation of the chapter, one must understand that the main question that was asked by the disciples and answered by Jesus in verses 4-28 was, "When will these things be?" The issue is the destruction of the temple. Verses 4-28 are all about the AD 70 destruction of Jerusalem and its temple and the great tribulation of Israel at that time. The gospel of Mark and Luke do not even mention the secondary questions, *"And what will be the sign of Your coming (parousia), and of the end of the age."* It is utterly shameful and irresponsible exegesis when many writers, preachers, and teachers almost, if not totally, ignore this primary question and interpret this chapter as though it were never asked. The entire chapter is supposedly about the second question regarding Jesus' return.

Unfortunately, most interpreters ignore two obvious factors, which confirm that verses 4-28 contain Jesus' answer to the first question.

1. This is a <u>private conversation</u> with four of His disciples, Peter, James, John, and Andrew (Mark 13:3). Jesus persistently addressed them with the personal pronoun *"you,"* thereby affirming that they would witness and be involved in these happenings;

this destruction of the temple and the great tribulation would occur in their lifetime. His concern was for them. He began by alerting them, *"See to it that no one misleads you (vs. 4)"* and *"see that you are not frightened (vs. 6)."* This use of the personal pronoun occurs in verses 2, 4, 6, 9, 15, 20, 23, 25 and 26 to link all of the events to the apostle's lifetime.

2.   Throughout this section Jesus makes <u>periodic time statements</u> that also tie all the forecast events to the lifetime of the apostles and the destruction of the temple.All the events listed in verses 4-8 are commonly taught as being signs of the end of the age and our Lord's return: false Christs, wars, and rumors of wars, famine, and earthquakes. Jesus said that these things are *"not yet the end"* (of the temple, let alone the end of the age); they represent only *"the beginning of birth pangs,"* and the event to be born will be the destruction of the temple. It is abundantly clear that Jesus said His disciples would witness all these events (vs. 6).

3.   In verses 9-14, Jesus then outlined another list of events that would soon occur—the tribulation and martyrdom of His disciples, the falling away of many, false prophets, lawlessness, love growing cold, and the preaching of the gospel in the world. Jesus made it very clear again when these things would happen. Verse 9 again places these events during the lifetime of the apostles. The word *"then"* confirms that they would occur during the same time period as the events noted in verses 4-8. He said that all the events named in verses 10-14 would occur *"at that time,"* that is, when the apostles would be tribulated and martyred (vs.9). Many mistakenly cite verse 14 as a prerequisite to the Lord's return and quickly point to the necessity of preaching the gospel to the whole world as proof that verses 4-14 and the following are about His return. They do not believe that the gospel had been proclaimed in all the world by the time the temple was destroyed. However, the Scriptures affirm otherwise. The apostles were given the responsibility to take the gospel into *"all the nations (Mt. 28:19)"* and subsequently filled with the Holy Spirit to witness *"to the remotest part of the earth (Ac. 1:8)."* Four separate texts announce that their mission was fulfilled in the lifetime of the apostles before the destruction of the temple in AD 70—Colossians 1:1-6, "We always thank God, the Father of our Lord Jesus Christ, when we pray for you, because we have heard of your faith in Christ Jesus and of the love you have for all God's people— the faith and love that spring from the hope stored up for you in heaven and about which you have already heard in the true message of the gospel that has come to you. In the same way, the gospel is bearing fruit and

growing if you continue in your faith, established and firm, and do not move from the hope held out in the gospel." Verse 23: "This is the gospel that you heard and that <u>has been proclaimed to every creature under heaven,</u> and of which I, Paul, have become a servant <u>throughout the whole world</u>—just as it has been doing among you since the day you heard it and truly understood God's grace. Then in Romans 1:8 "First, I thank my God through Jesus Christ for all of you, because your faith is being reported <u>all over the world</u>" and in 10:18: "But I ask: 'Did they not hear? Of course they did: "Their voice has gone out <u>into all the earth, their words to the ends of the world</u>."

4. It's Timing
Jesus clearly established the timing of the great tribulation of Israel to be when His apostles will have seen the abomination of desolation foretold by Daniel (Mt. 24:15; Dan. 9:26-27) and Jerusalem surrounded by armies (Lie. 21:20), which resulted in the destruction of Jerusalem and the temple in AD 70. The great tribulation, then, is already past; the prophecy of Jesus has been fulfilled. There is nothing in His words to warrant interpreting this prophecy as awaiting a future fulfillment unless one rewrites Jesus' words or, as many do, ignores their obvious meanings. The timing was at the heart of the disciples' question about the future. *"When will these things be..." (Mt. 24:3).* Jesus answered their question carefully and fully.

5. Its Nature
In addition to carefully establishing the timing of the temple's destruction and the accompanying great tribulation, Jesus made four significant revelations about the tribulation.
   a. It was a <u>local Jewish tribulation</u>. There is nothing to suggest a general universal tribulation. This is clearly stated in Luke 21:23-24, *"There will be great distress (trib.) upon the land (Judah), and wrath to this people (Israel)... they shall fall by the sword (war) and led captive into all nations."* Jesus concern was for *"those who are in Judea" (Mt. 24:16).*
   b. It was to be <u>the greatest ever</u> tribulation of Israel. It would be *"such as has not occurred since the beginning of the world until now..." (Mt. 24:21).* That statement ties it to Jeremiah's prophecy, *"It is the time of Jacob's distress (trib.)."* That prophecy was also fulfilled at that time for Jeremiah predicted a great day of which he said, *"There is none like it."*

    c.   The fact that it was the greatest ever tribulation of Israel also affirms that it will have <u>no future fulfillment</u>.

Some pretribulationalists and others have seen that the evidence is so overwhelming that they must admit that Matthew 24:4-28 was fulfilled in the AD 70 destruction of Jerusalem. However, they want to retain their unwarranted belief in a future seven-year tribulation, and they need this text to support that error, so they claim a double fulfillment for this prophecy. Two factors disallow that claim.

We do not have Scriptural authority to claim a double fulfillment for any prophecy.

Some cite Old Testament prophecies that seemed to have double fulfillments. Only one comes to my mind, that is Isaiah 11:14 *"a virgin shall conceive, etc."* That had an immediate and a future fulfillment. However, that was acknowledged and revealed in and by the Scriptures themselves to have a double fulfillment. Dare we decide and assign a second fulfillment to any prophecies not clearly designated by Scripture to have a second fulfillment? I, for one, do not believe so. Frankly, I do not trust myself to decide which ones do and which ones do not have a second fulfillment; nor do I trust anyone else to do so.

In this case, the question of whether some prophecies can have a double fulfillment and whether we have the authority to assign a second fulfillment to any prophecy is moot. JESUS HAS TOLD US THAT THERE WILL NOT BE A SECOND FULFILLMENT OF THIS PROPHECY! Jesus said that this would not only be a great tribulation, but THE GREATEST EVER for Israel. It will be and was *"Such as has not occurred since the beginning of the world until now, NOR EVER SHALL (BE AGAIN)!!! (Mt. 24:21).* There could be two great tribulations, but there cannot be two greatest ever tribulations. Thus, there is no future great tribulation predicted in this passage for Israel or the church. You can take Jesus' word on that!

While the greatest tribulation that occurred in AD 67-70 will not be repeated, Israel's tribulation will continue throughout this age. At that time, they were driven into all the nations where the majority of the Jews living today are still to be found. Jesus said, "Jerusalem will be trampled underfoot by the Gentiles until the time of the Gentiles be fulfilled" (Lk. 21:24), which will not be until Jesus returns.

Remember the dispensational interpretation of scripture; if it is clear, accept it as written. Is this clear?

J. DOES THE MESSAGE OF SCRIPTURE TEACH ESCAPE OR STEADFASTNESS?

Just because we have not seen much persecution in the USA does not mean it is non-existent. A specific 7-year "great tribulation" is another one of the issues concocted by the pre-tribulation rapture system to support their theology. Please note the clear wording of Revelation 7: 13, 14: "And one of the elders answered, saying unto me, 'These that are arrayed in the white robes, who are they, and whence came they?' And I say unto him, 'My lord, thou knowest.' And he said to me, 'These are they that come out of the great tribulation, and they washed their robes, and made them white in the blood of the Lamb.'" They endured, not escaped!

I continually ask you to think. Just think about this proposed secret rapture and its effect on the world. In a moment, in the twinkling of an eye, millions are missing, and there are no bodily remains. With Christians in control, planes crash, all at the same time, there are thousands of traffic accidents because there was no driver in the car, doctors and nurses are gone in medical facilities, some probably in the middle of surgery or urgent care, business owners and staff disappear amid sales transactions, bankers are gone, etc. How many more examples do we need? I was always taught that once Jesus came, there was no longer a possibility for salvation because the Holy Spirit was removed, and he is the one who convicts of sin. Wouldn't this be like the days of Noah when he went into the ark, God closed the door, the rains came, and all of the unbelievers were now convinced, but it was too late, and they perished?

Because of all of this, my logical mind convinces me that the rapture and the second coming are the same, and they come after tribulation.

Recently, I came upon a new concept. I had not heard this one before. This person says it is confirmed that Jesus died and was resurrected in 38AD. Two thousand years from then, January 2038, has to be the time he comes again. If he doesn't, this whole thing is a hoax, and he's really not coming again!!!! Really? Here we go again!

K. CONCLUSION ON THE GREAT TRIBULATION

The great tribulation of Israel, as prophesied by Daniel 9:26-27 and by Jesus in Matthew 24:4-28 is now past, having occurred in the AD 67-70 destruction of Jerusalem and its temple. The greatest ever aspect of it is in the past, but tribulation continues in milder forms from time to time and place to place while the Jews are scattered among the nations until the times of the Gentiles are fulfilled and the Lord returns (Lk. 21:24). And Jesus said, "That great tribulation will not ever occur again." (Mt. 24:21).

In conclusion, great scholars cannot agree. Someone must be incorrect. It could be me! Your position on eschatology is far less important than your preparedness for Christ's return whenever the Father chooses to send His Son. Be ready.

SECTION TWO: THE RETURN OF CHRIST

"And then shall they see the Son of Man coming in a cloud with power and great glory." (Luke 21:27)

Our world appears to be in upheaval in every arena. The Lord's last words on earth described the upheaval preceding His return. In this verse from Luke, two crucial words appear. "And then..." What are the signs that will announce His return? The disciples were eager to know the answer to this question. "Tell us, when shall these things be? And what shall be the sign of thy coming...?" (Matthew 24:3)

The Lord answered this question with an in-depth description of the events that would signal His coming. And He gave one clue in particular. He said the events would come like birth pangs that signal the birth of a baby. They begin slowly, build steadily, and finish in a flurry of final, painful agonies. Then the child appears. (John 16:21)

The Lord said, "When the Son of Man returns, it will be like it was in Noah's day. In those days before the Flood, the people were enjoying banquets and parties and weddings... People didn't realize what would happen until the flood swept them away." (Matthew 24:37-39 NLT) Noah had preached for 120 years before the Flood. He announced to them the prophetic Word of God. Yet these millions of people scoffed at rain since they had never seen it. The Apostle Peter describes this same attitude for the return of Christ. "Above all, you must understand that in the last days scoffers will come, scoffing and following their own evil desires." They will say, 'Where is this 'coming' he promised? Everything goes on since our ancestors died as it has since the beginning of creation.'" (II Peter 3:3,4) Then Peter issued a warning. "But do not forget this one thing, dear friends: With the Lord a day is like a thousand years, and a thousand years are like a day. The Lord is not slow in keeping his promise, as some understand slowness. Instead he is patient with you, not wanting anyone to perish, but everyone to come to repentance."

"But the day of the Lord will come like a thief. The heavens will disappear with a roar; the elements will be destroyed by fire, and the earth and everything done in it will be laid bare." (II Peter 3:8-10)

The Apostle Paul describes the world scene in "the latter times" also.

- Many will depart from true faith
- People will follow lying spirits (I Timothy 4:1,2)
- People will love only themselves
- People will love their money
- Disobedience to parents will abound
- People will be ungrateful
- Nothing will be considered sacred
- Lack of love and forgiveness evident
- No self-control
- Cruelty
- Reckless and proud
- Evil people and imposters will flourish
  (II Timothy 3:1-13 NLT)

Again, in Romans 1:24-30 Paul describes a world that will not be looking for Christ's return.

- Claiming to be wise, they are fools
- Doing whatever shameful things their heart desires
- Doing vile and degrading things sexually

Does this sound like the world as we see it today? The Lord tells us to look up as we see the signs because our "redemption draweth nigh." (Luke 21:28). We live in exciting times. The birth pangs are in process.

A. IS IT HONEST AND ACCURATE TO SAY THAT ALL PROPHECIES ARE FULFILLED PREDICTING THE SECOND COMING?

To be sure, many or most prophecies can be documented as fulfilled, but one of vital importance that does not seem so is that "all nations" will hear the gospel before Jesus returns. However, now I have a problem: I just told you the disciples fulfilled these verses! Matt. 24:14; Mark 13:10; Luke 24:47.

1. What is a nation? "There is a difference between the terms nation, state, and country, even though the words are often used interchangeably. Country and state are synonymous terms that both apply to self-governing political entities. A nation, however, is a group of people who share the same culture but do not have sovereignty. The word translated 'nations' is ἔθνος (ethnos), which is the word from which we derive the word 'ethnic.' It talks about ethnic communities, which we might call people groups today, not political states." (Bible Dictionary)

   We were always taught that in the Old Testament, various tribes were considered nations. Nomadic tribes had no boundaries. Were they nations? Have all people groups been reached? The issue is not how many have accepted the Bible message but how many have not even heard it.

   Oswald Smith famously said, "Why should some hear the gospel over and over again when others have not even heard it once?" or something similar. According to the Missionary Conference speaker representing the Christian and Missionary Alliance denomination, there are still 3.1 billion people unreached!

Today, we speak of these billions who have never heard, and yet some preachers say that all prophecies are fulfilled so that Christ could come at any moment. At that huge number, there must be some vast cultures or groups. And when defining nations as ethnic communities, are small tribes in the jungles not nations? They speak their own language and have their own currency and organizational structure (government?). But they have yet to hear! But the scripture says they will hear.

Rev. 5:9 "And they sang a new song, saying: 'You are worthy to take the scroll and to open its seals, because you were slain, and with your blood you purchased for God persons *from every tribe and language and people and nation.*'" (Note: every language.)

Rev. 14:6 "Then I saw another angel flying in midair, and he had the eternal gospel to proclaim to those who live on the earth—*to every nation, tribe, language and people.*" (Note the terminology.)

2. How do we resolve the problem?

    Following Jesus and the disciples, and in the years to follow, we hear this from scripture: we are not off the hook, and the gospel must continue to be spread.

    Acts 1:8: "But you will receive power when the Holy Spirit comes on you; and you will be my witnesses in Jerusalem, and in all Judea and Samaria, and to the ends of the earth." These are the last words of Jesus.

    Romans 10:14: "How, then, can they call on the one they have not believed in? And how can they believe in the one of whom they have not heard? And how can they hear without someone preaching to them?"

    II Cor. 5:20: "We are therefore Christ's ambassadors, as though God were making his appeal through us. We implore you on Christ's behalf: Be reconciled to God."

    See also Acts 8:4; Col. 4:5,6; I Cor. 9 22,23; I Pet. 3:15.

3. Reaching every tribe and nation before Christ returns just got a tremendous boost. I do not know all the specifics and have many questions. Indeed, this is an enormous leap in the spread of the gospel."

The Internet's Final Frontier: Remote Amazon Tribes." The New York Times. June 2, 2024. Ronald Barn

"Jack Nicas and Victor Moriyama, two *The New York Times* reporters, hiked more than 50 miles through the Amazon to reach remote Marubo villages...to see what happened to villagers who had just received a Starlink satellite internet antenna... which 'connected' the tiny, closed civilization, among the most remote indigenous villages on the planet, to the rest of us...courtesy of Elon Musk's SpaceX. The benefits of 'video chats with faraway loved ones and calls for help in emergencies' are obvious... 'please don't take our Internet away,' the female leader of one village plaintively asked the reporters.

"SpaceX's current two most important businesses are 'Starlink' and 'Launch.' Starlink is a satellite broadband Internet service. Starlink's satellite broadband serves the entire Planet Earth from its 6,500 low earth orbital (LEO), low latency satellites.

"...We think of SpaceX as the 'railroad to space' ... and analogize SpaceX rockets to America's railroads in the late 1800s. Railroads enabled our nation to settle America's West. Railroads then were a dramatic improvement over wagon trains. Just like reflyable rockets are a dramatic improvement over expensive rockets that can be used only once. No other commercial enterprise or government has been able to refly rockets...which, when you watch SpaceX landings, you too will quickly understand why it is such an awesome feat.

"Approximately 90% of the mass to orbit from Planet Earth is currently launched by SpaceX. Elon estimates that when SpaceX Starship, the 400-foot tall, largest rocket ever launched from our planet, has been 'derisked,' 99% of all mass to orbit will be flown by SpaceX! Whether for commercial interests or governments."

How soon can all tribes receive these satellite antennas? Who will know the languages of those who have never been reached? Is there a ministry or company that understands the technology, and how much does it cost?

All these and more questions must be answered and addressed, but undeniably, this is a giant leap to meeting the requirement that all tribes and nations will hear the gospel before the Lord returns.

Given the above, is it honest to say that nothing needs to be fulfilled to hinder Christ's imminent return?

B. THE FINAL WAR

Armageddon in Hebrews means hill of slaughter.

RUSSIA AND HER ALLIES WILL ATTACK ISRAEL...Pastor Larry Burd

Ezekiel 38:1-12, especially 7-8: "Get ready; be prepared, you and all the hordes gathered about you, and take command of them. After many days you will be called to arms. In future years you will invade a land... Israel."

Russia and her allies will attack Israel. See the following verses: Rev. 16:12-16; James 4:1,2; Rev. 12:7-9 (first war); Matt. 24:6; Zach. 13:8:14 (nuclear war???): Rev. 14:9,10; Rev. 19:11 (greatest victory).

Old Testament names for nations and their present names:

1. Gog = a general title for an enemy of God's people. Could apply to any number of nations/people.
2. Magog = land of the prince. Here is the prophecy against Gog and Magog: Ezekiel 39:1,2; Genesis 10:2; Revelation 20:7-10
3. Rosh = means head. Here are the prophecies for the coalition of nations: Ezekiel 27:10, 13-14; Nahum 3:9; Ezekiel 37: 20-27.
4. Meshech = Moscow. Meshech and Tubal mean "head."
5. Persia = Iran (since 1935)
6. Cush = Ethopia.
7. Put = Libya.
8. Gomer = Germany.
9. Beth-Togermaa = Eastern Turkey.

Would you agree that the nations are in alignment today as they never were before?

C. THE END OF THE WORLD

"The end of the world is coming soon..."
~ I Peter 4:7 (NLT)

Many people today easily dismiss the idea that "the end of the world is coming soon." One argument is that people have been saying that forever, and we are still here. And, of course, the Apostle Peter said that in his letter, written two thousand years ago.

So, what are we to believe as believers in the 21st Century? Well, we must begin with the fact that the Word of God clearly teaches that there is a day coming when the world as we know it will come to an explosive end.

Peter wrote, "First, I want to remind you that in the last days there will be scoffers ... This will be their argument: 'Jesus promised to come back, did he? Then where is he? Why, as far back as anyone can remember, everything has remained exactly the same since the world was first created ... But the day of the Lord will come as unexpectedly as a thief. Then the heavens will pass away with a terrible noise, and everything in them will disappear in fire, and the earth and everything in it will be exposed to judgment." (II Peter 3:3, 4, 10 NLT)

Christ Himself clearly taught the disciples that there would be a final end of the world as we know it. "... there will be famines and earthquakes ... But all this will be only the beginning of the horrors to come ... Sin will be rampant everywhere ... finally, the end will come... Heaven and earth will disappear." (Matthew 24:7, 8, 12, 14, 35 NLT)

The Word of God gives consistent warnings of coming judgment. In the days of Noah, the Lord warned that the end of the world as it existed at that time was coming. And, in about 2400 B.C., the entire human civilization was destroyed, with the exception of eight people.

When the Lord warned Sodom and Gomorrah that their world was ending, only three people escaped. All the rest died in fiery explosions.

When Jesus spoke to the disciples and the Jewish population of 33 A.D., He told them of the coming destruction of the world as they knew it. Israel would be destroyed. Jerusalem would be ravaged. And their glorious Temple would be taken apart, stone by stone. "Do you see all these buildings? I assure you, they will be so completely demolished that not one stone will be left on top of another." (Matthew 24:2 NLT) Less than forty years later the Roman army, in 70 A.D., marched into Israel and killed millions of Jews and destroyed the Temple, melting the stones down to gain the gold coverings.

We, too, in the 21st Century, have the Word of God that clearly outlines the signs of the end of the world as we know it. There will be famines, earthquakes, wars, rumors of wars, wickedness of every kind, economic disaster, and a rejection of the Word of God. "In the last days there will be very difficult times. For people will love only themselves and their money. They will be ... scoffing at God, disobedient to their parents, and ungrateful." (II Timothy 3:1, 2 NLT)

Certainly, today, we see all of the above and much more outlined in His Word. What is our response to be as believers? First, we must be very well-informed in the Word of God. Generally speaking, religious Jews of the first century completely dismissed Jesus Christ as the Messiah because they did not believe or understand prophecy, even though they had access to the Scripture. Secondly, we are to be fearless, living boldly for Christ. We know in Whom we have believed, and therefore, we are to walk in peace. "God has not given us a spirit of fear ... but of power and love." (II Timothy 1:7 NLT) And, finally, we are to tell others of Jesus Christ. Only those in Christ will escape the coming judgment of our world. "So you must never be ashamed to tell others about our Lord... with the strength God gives you, be ready to suffer with me for the proclamation of the Good News." (II Timothy 1:8 NLT)

We are living in exciting days. We are to look up! Our Redeemer "draweth nigh." (Luke 21:28)

Lord, give us anointed eyes to grasp the truth of Your Word as it applies to these days in which we live.

D. WHAT IF THE USA IS NOT IN GOD'S PLAN FOR THE FUTURE?

I often urge you to think, but I, too, am thinking, and the thoughts forming are unsettling.

I am not a prophet, and I did not have a particular word from God. I am simply synthesizing my thoughts concerning the influence of the United States in God's plan for end times. These have been with me for many years but seem to be coming together. Will you think with me?

Despite the efforts of Bible scholars over the years, the United States is notably absent from the last days in scripture. Many nations are mentioned, including Egypt, Russia, China, Turkey, Iran, Iraq, and Libya. But the USA is not among them.

We always say that scripture is precise. All details are covered minutely. If so, how could the most powerful nation on earth be missing in end-time prophecy? Did God forget? Is it just because we did not exist when the Bible was written? I don't think so.

So, are we going to make America great again? Or is it possible that God is setting the stage for the implosion of our great nation as a part of His plan? Why would God make us great again apart from a massive revival? We are deteriorating morally. God punished His people, Israel, many times because of their disobedience, and here we are, becoming like Sodom and Gomorrah.

We devote special times and days of prayer, pray personally for the nation, post signs, place ads, and do all sorts of things, asking for His blessing. But why would He bless us when even some Christians vote for a political party that champions abortion, homosexuality, same-sex marriage, etc.? Why would He bless us when our lifestyles are so similar to the world's that non-Christians cannot tell the difference?

We believe that the focal point of end-time prophecy is Israel. God will preserve her. Look at the present situation. Count the nations that have a stated desire to eradicate her. More and more, the youth in America are rioting against her. Hate crimes against Jews have risen more than 50% in the past year.

Is my thinking correct? I certainly hope not. I love America but cannot see us on the present path much longer. God cannot tolerate sin. He is longsuffering, but how long?

Here are just a small sampling of verses concerning the last days, the coming of Christ:

II Pet: 3:4 "They will say, "Where is this 'coming' he promised? Ever since our ancestors died, everything goes on as it has since the beginning of creation." Do we see this today in the USA?

I Pet. 4:7 "They will say, "The end of all things is near. Therefore be alert and of sober mind so that you may pray." We hear very little in our churches today about the coming of Christ. It used to be central to our thinking.

2 Peter 3:10 "But the day of the Lord will come like a thief. The heavens will disappear with a roar; the elements will be destroyed by fire, and the earth and everything done in it will be laid bare." The unprepared will be shocked.

II Tim. 3:1-5 "But mark this: There will be terrible times in the last days. People will be lovers of themselves, lovers of money, boastful, proud, abusive, disobedient to their parents, ungrateful, unholy, without love, unforgiving, slanderous, without self-control, brutal, not lovers of the good, treacherous, rash, conceited, lovers of pleasure rather than lovers of God— having a form of godliness but denying its power…" Does this describe our nation?

If these are the last days, and America is not mentioned in the last days, how much longer do we have?

I want to make absolutely certain that everyone understands these are **my** thoughts. They are not inspired! But I sincerely trust you will think about them and not simply read and forget. I would be overjoyed if someone gave me a rebuttal based on logic and the scriptures.

E. PRAYER

Lord, we know that Your Word is truth and Your nature is love. Let us embrace Your plan for ourselves and for the world You created. "Even so, come quickly, Lord Jesus." Revelation 22:20, 21

CHAPTER

7

SPECIAL DAYS

A. CHRISTMAS

1. What If He Hadn't Come?

A Pastor's Dream

A clergyman fell into a deep sleep in his office at church on Christmas Sunday morning before be like without Christmas...

- No Christmas stockings
- No Christmas bells
- No wreaths of holly
- No Christmas tree
- He walked out into the street...
- No church spire
- No decorations
- No beautiful Christmas music
- He came back in and looked at the books in his study...
- Every book about Jesus was gone

Just then, the doorbell rang, and a stranger asked him to visit with a weeping child.

There were no verses to comfort her, for they are all in the New Testament, and it was missing.

There is no gospel, no salvation, no resurrection, no promise for a life with Christ throughout eternity. All he could do was cry alongside her.

He suddenly awoke, and the church service had already begun. He heard, "Joy to the world, the Lord is come."

Jesus makes all of the difference.

2. A World Without Jesus

Has the thought ever crossed your mind of what the world would be like without Jesus? Think with me:

The land mass of North America would most likely be very different in culture and religion. South America and North America were both explored about the same time (1490-1550). They are essentially the same size in land mass and have approximately the same number of natural resources. But look at the difference between the two continents. Why? People went to South America to discover riches and gold; people came to North America to seek religious freedom. Have you ever thought through the difference in culture and progress between those nations that at least had access to the gospel and those that never heard it? They are called third-world nations for a reason! Think of the difference in countries that honor Jehovah as God—including Israel, the USA and Canada, most of Europe, Great Britain, etc. But in Third World nations, developing nations, there is absolute poverty (per capita annual income...16 countries under $1000); serious health issues (life expectancy...48-60); political rights and civil liberties almost non-existent (dictators massacre hundreds of thousands); ethnic cleansing.

How would you like to be a woman in the OT? How would you want to be a woman living in the Middle East? How would you like to be a woman in many third-world countries today? How would you like to be committed to the next brother in line if your husband dies? But Jesus treated women differently. He initiated a conversation with the woman at the well, forgave the woman who was being stoned for adultery, and revealed himself to two women after his resurrection. Paul told men to love their wives as Christ loved the church and gave Himself for it!!!!!

How would you like to have been born in a communist country where they were told there is no God? Go to the former Soviet Union, and they are clamoring for God. Look at this country trying to get rid of God!

These are reasons why Jesus has made a difference wherever His Name has been spread.

No Jesus, no Christmas.

No New Testament.

If Jesus hadn't come, there would be no calendar as we know it, and for Old Testament time, B.C., it would still be operable. That means there would be no New Testament, which introduced Jesus and began our present A.D. calendar.

No New Testament would exist, and we would still live under Jewish law. The OT talks about the future salvation of the Gentiles and the NT talks about the fact of salvation at present. (Paul—Acts 18:5,6; Peter's vision—Acts 10:1—11:2, especially 10:45. See Galatians 3:8,9,14,28.) Animal sacrifices would still cover our sins because there would be no "once for all" sacrifice. (Hebrews 10:1,1,10).

Do you realize that there are only two non-Jews mentioned in the Old Testament? One was Rahab the harlot (who is in the line of Christ) and the other is Ruth (who followed the religion of her mother-in-law, Naomi).

The New Testament opens up the possibility of non-Jews having a relationship with Jehovah. There were millions of non-Jews before the coming of Christ but to them there was never a missionary to tell them about Jehovah…He was for the Jews alone; but when Christ came, he made salvation possible for all people.

Geneses 22:18: "And in thy seed shall all the nations of the earth be blessed; because thou hast obeyed my voice."

Isaiah 49:6: "And he said, 'It is a light thing that thou shouldest be my servant to raise up the tribes of Jacob, and to restore the preserved of Israel; I will also give thee for a light to the Gentiles that thou mayest be my salvation unto the ends of the earth.'"

Peter had a vision. Cornelius, an Italian officer in Caesarea, was a devoutly religious man. Even the Jews acknowledged him as a good man because of all he did for the people. One day, he had a vision. God told him to send for Peter, who was in Joppa. At about the same time, Peter had a vision. A sheet was let down to earth from the heavens, and animals and birds of all kinds were in it. Then a voice came from heaven, "Kill whatever you want and eat it." But Peter refused because he had never eaten anything that was not kosher, so God repeated the message three times. Peter woke up and asked God to tell him what the vision meant. Just then, the messengers from Cornelius showed up and asked Peter to go with them to Joppa. He agreed. Cornelius had gathered a group of Gentiles and asked Peter to speak to them. Peter was stunned and realized that the animals in the sheet meant that being able to eat all meat indicated that the Jewish message of the messiah could be shared with all people; it was not just for the Jews.

Imagine your life without the teachings of the New Testament being operable.

No Christmas, no New Testament.

Everyone has the same facts: everyone knows the Christmas story inside out. Some accept it as fact, while others sincerely believe it is a great feel-good story that is grossly overblown.

So, what makes the difference? It all lies in your approach to the miracles of Christ's birth. You will find it if you come with a humble, open heart desiring truth. If you come with questions soaked in prejudice, you will not.

What will you do with Jesus? It's up to you right now. Your eternity depends on it.

3. "You Came"

When they met, she was fifteen, and he was seventeen. They dated all through high school, so no one was surprised when they got married.

Some four years and two children later, she was standing in the kitchen with dirty dishes in the sink and dirty diapers in the corner. Tears were streaming down her face. Looking back, she could never be exactly sure why she made the decision, but she did make it. She took off her apron and walked out.

She called that night, and her young husband answered the phone. He was understandably quite worried and also quite angry.

"Where are you?" he demanded, his concern and anger fighting to control his voice.

"How are the children?" she asked, ignoring his question.

"Well, if you mean to ask if they are fed, they are. I've also put them to bed. They are wondering, just as I am, where you are and what you think you are doing."

She hung up that night, but it wasn't the last of the phone calls. She called every week for the next three months. Knowing something was seriously wrong, her husband began in those phone calls to plead with her to come home. He would tell her that the children were with their grandparents during the day and were well cared for. But he would also tell her that he loved her. He would tell her how much they all missed her, and then he tried to find out where she was. Whenever the conversation turned to her whereabouts, she hung up.

Finally, the young husband could stand it no longer. He took their savings and hired a private detective to find her. The detective found and reported her in a third-rate Des Moines, IA hotel.

The young man borrowed money from his in-laws, bought a plane ticket, and flew to Des Moines. After taking a cab from the airport to the hotel, he climbed the stairs to his wife's third-room floor. (Those kinds of hotels didn't have elevators.) If you had been there, you would have seen the doubt in his eyes and the perspiration on his forehead. His hand trembled as he knocked on the door.

When his wife opened the door, he forgot his prepared speech and simply said, "We love you so much. Won't you come home?"

She fell apart in his arms. They went home together.

Some weeks later, the children were in bed one evening, and he and his wife were sitting in the living room by the fire. He finally got up enough courage to ask the question that haunted him for many months: "Why wouldn't you come home? Why, when I told you repeatedly that I loved you and missed you, didn't you come home?"

"Because" she said with profound simplicity, "they were only words. But then you came."

And that's the story of Christmas. Through the centuries, God told His people how much He loved them. They left Him again and again, but He never gave up. Then, to prove His love, He sent His Son to walk and talk with them…and eventually to die for them.

Sent to love and to die. Redemption's story.

If you haven't already done so, go home with Him.

—Story told originally by Steve Brown

B. THANKSGIVING

1. Thankful For Things Easily Overlooked

I Cor: 5:18 "In everything give thanks: for this is the will of God in Christ Jesus concerning you." (KJV)

As I analyze my regular prayers, I realize that I do much more asking than thanking. Today I want to think about things I've grown accustomed to and take for granted.

First, I'm thankful for my health. I know from experience what it is like to wonder where I would get my next breath or whether my heart would stop. I know what it is like to be able to take what seems like every ounce of energy to put one foot in front of the other just to get across a room. I know what it is to be unable to stop a bloody nose, have it packed for 6 weeks, and breathe through my mouth. I'm thankful that I feel good again. I'm thankful that I can hear, see, and have a reasonably sound mind at an advanced age.

I'm thankful that I live in a comfortable apartment—bricks and mortar and a roof. I'm thankful for a/c and heat, a refrigerator and stove, and a comfortable bed. I realize that over 1,000,000 people live in just ten of the largest refugee camps in the world, and there are hundreds of smaller ones growing daily.

I'm thankful for fresh water to drink. I've traveled enough to know what a nuisance it is to depend on purchasing bottled water, even to brush my teeth. They tell me that over 633,000,000 around the world drink polluted water.

I'm thankful for enough food to eat. Although it is estimated that 12% of the world's population dies of starvation yearly, here I am with at least 10 varieties of every food you can imagine!

I'm thankful for my toilet. It sounds silly to be grateful for that, but I am. I've seen with my own eyes people defecating outdoors and statistics say that about 940,000,000 around the world do this.

I'm thankful for the sufficient income that I do not have to worry about meeting my expenses. I remember what it was like when we had a bank account that didn't even have $10 in it by the end of the month, and I got paid once a month!

I'm thankful for our marriage. We have not only survived but enjoyed 66 years together, and we never had one minute of pre-marital counseling! We have seen your hand in our lives repeatedly. Talk about being blessed...!

I'm thankful for my family. I know we made many mistakes along the way, but by your grace, they all love you and each other! Thank you for changing my heart from critical to sensitive for those parents who have not experienced the same results even though they did their best. You were particularly gracious to us.

I'm thankful for the privilege of public ministry for more than 60 years. I'm thankful for the people I met who helped shape my life...and for the input I have rendered to many others.

There are so many more things if space would allow. My country, my church, my friends....

Lastly, and most importantly, thank you for my salvation. It indeed is a marvelous gift from you. And thanks for the incredible future I have with you for eternity.

"If you can't be thankful for what you receive, be thankful for what you escape." Anonymous

2. Saying Thanks

Psalms 100:4 "Enter his gates with thanksgiving and his courts with praise; give thanks to him and praise his name."

Approximately 64 years ago, on the coast-to-coast Youth on the March Thanksgiving telecast, Steve Musto, a dear friend, recited a poem. I have been searching for it for the past 50 years when I had to preach or teach at Thanksgiving. By sheer coincidence(!!!), I found it in a book on my bookshelf. The book in which I found it simply says "selected," so I do not know the author.

You know the story of the ten lepers healed by Jesus, and only one returned to say thanks. (Luke 17: 12-19)

Don't just read these words. Mentally dress yourself as a leper and sense the deep, passionate remorse of being instantly cleansed from disease, isolation, and scorn and not even saying thanks. Read with a trembling voice of guilt and sorrow, as must have been the case with this one healed leper who admitted he missed the opportunity to thank Jesus personally, face-to-face. Imagine yourself on coast-to-coast TV presenting this as Steve did many years ago. That is what I "see" in my mind.

The Remorse of the Nine Ungrateful Lepers

"I meant to go back, but you may guess
I was filled with amazement I cannot express
To think for those horrible years,
That passion and loathing and passion of fears,
For sores unendurable-eaten, defiled-
My flesh was as smooth as the flesh of a child.
I was drunken with joy; I was crazy with glee;
I scarcely could walk and I scarcely could see,
For the dazzle of sunshine where all had been black;
But I meant to go back, Oh, I meant to go back!
I had thought to return, when my people came out,
There were tears of rejoicing and laughter and shout;
My cup was so full I seemed nothing to lack-
But I meant to go back, Oh, I meant to go back!"

How thankful are we? How much do we take for granted? Does it not seem that the more we have, the less we are thankful? Or even worse, the more we get out of the goodness of people's generosity, the more we expect.

I accompanied my boss in delivering a Christmas turkey to a "needy" family and arriving at the door; we were loudly told to come in by a man who never moved, sitting in a stuffed chair in a tee shirt with a can of beer at 10 AM in a beastly hot room. Upon seeing the turkey we were carrying and never looking away from the TV he was watching, he said, "Put it on the table." We wished him a Merry Christmas and left. He never acknowledged us correctly and indeed indicated no appreciation whatsoever.

While this may be extreme, how many people receive many good gifts and never say a meaningful thank you?

Is it time that you and I carefully examine our past and return to some significant "something" for which we have never shown sufficient gratitude? Maybe this is the lesson of Thanksgiving this year?

I wonder how many people we know who consider themselves Christians will sit at a Thanksgiving feast and never say a prayer of thanks to the Lord. I don't mean a recited prayer, which has become routine and meaningless; I mean a sincere thank you, realizing how many millions around the world are starving at this very moment.

Will you say, "I meant to go back, Oh, I meant to go back," or will you actually do what you must to go back and say thanks? Perhaps you could begin by reading the passage of scripture and acting out the poem above before eating your meal.

Psalm 106:1 "Praise the Lord. Give thanks to the Lord, for he is good; his love endures forever."

C. FOURTH OF JULY

Independence Day

How grateful I am to God that I am an American. Now we celebrate our independence on the Fourth of July.

Did you know that the Declaration of Independence was signed on July 2nd, not July 4th, and not in Philadelphia as in the famous painting? Also interesting is that two former presidents died on the 4th, Thomas Jefferson and John Adams (actually hours apart!), and one was born on this day, Calvin Coolidge.

The Statue of Liberty is a figure of Libertas, a robed Roman liberty goddess. She holds a torch above her head with her right hand, and in her left-hand carries a tabula ansata inscribed JULY IV MDCCLXXVI (July 4, 1776, in Roman numerals), the date of the U.S. Declaration of Independence. A broken shackle and chain lie at her feet as she walks forward, commemorating the recent national abolition of slavery. After its dedication, the statue became an icon of freedom and of the United States, seen as a symbol of welcome to immigrants arriving by sea.

Neil Enloe wrote a wonderful song about it and its connection to our salvation. He and the Couriers sang this many times at Sandy Cove in our concerts, and the Choralaires and brass ensemble featured it one summer with Beth (Lonie, daughter of the famed Don Lonie) Bradshaw as soloist.

Statue of Liberty

In New York Harbor stands a lady with a torch raised to the sky,
And all who see her know she stands for liberty for you and me.
I'm so proud to be called an American, to be named with the brave and the free.
I will honor our flag and our trust in God, and the Statue of Liberty.

On lonely Golgotha stood a cross, with my Lord raised to the sky,
And all who kneel there live forever as all the saved can testify.
I'm so glad to be called a Christian, to be named with the ransomed and whole.
As the statue liberates the citizen, so the cross liberates the soul.

Oh, the cross is my statue of liberty, it was there that my soul was set free.
Unashamed I'll proclaim that a rugged cross is my statue of liberty.

John 8:36: "So if the Son sets you free, you will be free indeed."

We need to pray for America in these days when the flag is being desecrated and burned and where Christianity is being mocked and shunned.

Psalm 33:12: "Blessed is the nation whose God is the Lord…"

God bless America.

D. EASTER

1. Is the Resurrection Necessary?

Romans 10:9,10: "If you declare with your mouth, 'Jesus is Lord,' and believe in your heart that God raised him from the dead, you will be saved. For it is with your heart that you believe and are justified, and it is with your mouth that you profess your faith and are saved."

I Corinthians 15:17: "And if Christ has not been raised, *your faith is futile*; you are still in your sins."

There are 106 quotes from the Bible concerning the resurrection and related issues, according to https://www.openbible.info/topics/resurrection.

Therefore, I must conclude that the resurrection is vital to God's heart. To deny it is to deny what the Bible teaches so clearly that it leaves no room for question or interpretation.

I have two friends who travel to the Holy Land. One claims to have the best tour guide and has used him for 36 trips, and the other claims that his tour guide is rated as the number two guide (who is female), though his trips are less frequent. Both friends say that if either of the guides stood up to give an evangelistic message, they can quote scripture with the best preachers and present an excellent case for Jesus as Messiah. But neither believes in the resurrection. Therefore, I must conclude that they are not born again. My friends agree.

Further, if we are to spend eternity in heaven, we must be raised from the grave and resurrected. And that is precisely what the Bible promises.

Ephesians 4:7-10: "But to each one of us grace has been given as Christ apportioned it. This is why it says "When he ascended on high, he took many captives and gave gifts to his people." (What does "he ascended" mean except that he also descended to the lower, earthly regions[c]? He who descended is the very one who ascended higher than all the heavens, in order to fill the whole universe.)

In I Corinthians 15:20-23 we read, "But Christ has indeed been raised from the dead, the firstfruits of those who have fallen asleep. For since death came through a man, the resurrection of the dead comes also through a man. For as in Adam all die, so in Christ all will be made alive. But each in turn: Christ, the firstfruits; then, when he comes, those who belong to him."

Let's unwrap that. In Luke 16, we read the story of the rich man and Lazarus. The beggar died and was carried off to Abraham's bosom. The rich man also died and went to Hades and was in torment. A "great gulf fixed" was between Hades and Abraham's bosom. This teaches us that heaven was not yet available to man. Jesus died, was resurrected, ascended into heaven, the first one to enter (the first fruits), and carried all who had previously been in Abraham's bosom with Him. It also indicates that those yet awaiting their final destination in Hades will be cast into the lake of fire, hell. In Revelation 20:13 we read, "And I saw the dead, great and small, standing before the throne, and books were opened. Another book was opened, which is the book of life. The dead were judged according to what they had done as recorded in the books. The sea gave up the dead that were in it, and death and Hades gave up the dead that were in them, and each person was judged according to what they had done. Then death and Hades were thrown into the lake of fire. The lake of fire is the second death. Anyone whose name was not found written in the book of life was thrown into the lake of fire."

Concerning man's resurrection of believers, other texts say:

I Corinthians 6:14: "By his power God raised the Lord from the dead, and he will raise us also."

II Corinthians 4:14: "because we know that the one who raised the Lord Jesus from the dead will also raise us with Jesus and present us with you to himself."

I Corinthians 15:51-53: "Listen, I tell you a mystery: We will not all sleep, but we will all be changed—in a flash, in the twinkling of an eye, at the last trumpet. For the trumpet will sound, the dead will be raised imperishable, and we will be changed. For the perishable must clothe itself with the imperishable, and the mortal with immortality."

The theme of resurrection is the core of Christianity. It is vital. Anything less is eternally fatal.

E. CONCLUSION

These are my thoughts. I want to emphasize again that others who love the Lord as much as I do have thoughts different than mine. I have searched the scriptures personally and used my experiences, both good and bad, to come to these conclusions. My desire for this book is to make you think for yourself. If you disagree and base the disagreement on your personal studies, I will have achieved my goal.

Printed in the United States
by Baker & Taylor Publisher Services